Grammar, Usage, and Mechanics Book

McDougal Littell

GRADE ELEVEN

Teaching

More Practice

Application

McDougal Littell

A HOUGHTON MIFFLIN COMPANY

Evanston, Illinois   Boston   Dallas

ISBN-13: 978-0-618-30394-6   ISBN-10: 0-618-30394-4

11– CKI –08 07

Contents

Special Features

The *Grammar, Usage, and Mechanics Workbook* contains a wealth of skill-building exercises.

Each lesson has different levels of worksheets. **Teaching** introduces the skill; **More Practice** and **Application** extend the skill with advanced exercises.

Worksheets correspond to lessons in the Pupil's Edition.

Each page focuses on one topic or skill. A brief instructional summary on the **Teaching** page is followed by reinforcement activities.

Key words and phrases are highlighted for greater clarity and ease of use.

When appropriate, example sentences demonstrate how to complete exercises.

Tabs make it easy to navigate the book.

Name _____   Date _____

Lesson 2

Appositive Phrases   *Teaching*

An **appositive** is a noun or pronoun that identifies or renames another noun or pronoun. An **appositive phrase** consists of an appositive plus its modifiers.

> Have you heard of the writer <u>Lydia Maria Child</u>? (*Lydia Maria Child* identifies *the writer.*)

> Her best-known work, <u>a poem that begins "Over the river and through the woods,"</u> was set to music. (The appositive phrase is underlined.)

An **essential appositive** make the meaning of a sentence clear.

> The abolitionist <u>Child</u> wrote to end slavery. (*Child* identifies which *abolitionist.*)

A **nonessential appositive** adds extra information to a sentence whose meaning is already clear. Use commas to set off nonessential appositive phrases.

> She is also known for starting a magazine for children, <u>the first of its kind</u>.

A. Identifying Appositives and Appositive Phrases

Underline the appositive or appositive phrase in each of the following sentences.

1. The American author Henry David Thoreau lived for a time at Walden Pond.
2. Paula wrote about Edgar Allan Poe, the American poet and short-story writer.
3. John Steinbeck, author of *The Grapes of Wrath,* was raised in California.
4. "God Bless America" was written by the prolific and patriotic composer Irving Berlin.
5. Nathaniel Hawthorne and his friends began their own community, Brook Farm.
6. Will Rogers, a humorist and philosopher, was originally a cowboy.
7. American poet Theodore Roethke received a Pulitzer Prize in 1954.
8. Harriet Beecher Stowe's novel *Uncle Tom's Cabin* describes slavery in the years before the American Civil War.

B. Identifying Essential and Nonessential Appositives

Underline the appositive or appositive phrase in each sentence below. On the line, identify each phrase as **E** if it is essential or **NE** if it is nonessential. Add the necessary commas to sentences with nonessential clauses.

1. The poetry of Robert Frost is identified with rural New England the place where Frost was raised.   _____

2. *Spin a Soft Black Song* a book of poetry for young readers was written by Nikki Giovanni.   _____

3. Katherine Lee Bates wrote the patriotic hymn "America the Beautiful" after viewing the Rocky Mountains.   _____

4. Author and journalist Louis Bromfield lived part of his life on a farm in Ohio.   _____

5. The running of the bulls in Pamplona, Spain, was described in Hemingway's book *Death in the Afternoon.*   _____

CHAPTER 2

Review 1 **Nouns**   *Teaching*

A noun is a word that names a person, place, thing, or idea.

Type of noun	Definition	Example
common noun	general name for a person, place, thing, or idea	city
proper noun	name of a particular person, place, thing, or idea	Baltimore
singular noun	one person, place, thing, or idea	street
plural noun	more than one person, place, thing, or idea	streets
collective noun	name of a group regarded as a unit	council
concrete noun	name of something perceptible by the senses	sign
abstract noun	name of an idea, quality, or state	law
compound noun	single noun formed from two or more words	streetlight
possessive noun	noun that shows ownership or relationship	dog's tail, dogs' tails

Finding Nouns

Underline every noun in each sentence.

1. Most of the people in the world live in cities.
2. Cities offer a number of opportunities for their citizens, from jobs to entertainment.
3. Every city offers its own special attractions.
4. Usually, a city is known for at least one unique landmark.
5. In Philadelphia, look for Independence Hall where the Declaration of Independence was signed.
6. Most older towns developed near a body of water, such as the ocean, or a river or lake.
7. Cleveland, Ohio, grew up by Lake Erie, a waterway that gave local industries a way to transport materials and products.
8. What factors determine a typical citizen's choice of which city to call home?
9. Weather may play a part in the choice.
10. Many Americans say that they enjoy the warm, dry weather of the Southwest.
11. Other people choose a hometown based on factors such as the presence of a professional sports team.
12. What attracts residents to your hometown?
13. Perhaps your city has many museums, galleries, and libraries where you can spend a quiet Sunday.
14. Could the attraction be the scenery or the schools?
15. In the past, some cities such as Reims, France, were built inside protective walls.
16. The wall was designed to discourage invaders.
17. The cities of Europe usually had one main church that towered over the rest of the buildings.
18. Skyscrapers dominate the skyline of the modern city.
19. Noisy traffic often clogs the streets, especially at rush hour.
20. Do you enjoy the excitement and fast pace of urban life?

Review 1 Nouns

More Practice

A. Identifying Nouns

Identify each numbered and italicized noun by writing **common, proper, abstract, concrete, collective, compound,** or **possessive** on the corresponding line below. Each noun belongs to at least two categories.

The stretch of **(1)** *Hudson Street* where I live is each day the scene of an intricate sidewalk **(2)** *ballet.* I make my own first entrance into it a little after eight when I put out the garbage can, surely a prosaic **(3)** *occupation,* but I enjoy my part, my little **(4)** *clang,* as the **(5)** *droves* of junior high school students walk by the center of the stage dropping candy wrappers. (How do they eat so much candy so early in the morning?)

While I sweep up the wrappers I watch the other rituals of the morning: Mr. Halpert unlocking the laundry's **(6)** *handcart* from its mooring to a cellar door, Joe Comacchia's **(7)** *son-in-law* stacking out the empty crates from the delicatessen, the barber bringing out his sidewalk folding chair, . . . I exchange my ritual **(8)** *farewell* with Mr. Lofaro, the short, thick-bodied, white-aproned fruit man who stands outside his **(9)** *doorway* a little up the street, his arms folded, his feet planted, looking as solid as earth itself. We nod; we each glance quickly up and down the street, then look back to each other and smile. We have done this many a morning for more than ten **(10)** *years,* and we both know what it means: All is well.

Jane Jacobs, *The Death and Life of Great American Cities*

1. _____   6. _____

2. _____   7. _____

3. _____   8. _____

4. _____   9. _____

5. _____   10. _____

B. Identifying Nouns

Underline the noun or nouns described in parentheses after each sentence.

1. Antonio emigrated to the United States from Italy. (proper noun)
2. The homeless woman in the doorway often reads the newspaper. (common noun)
3. The bicycle had a basket attached to the handlebars. (common noun)
4. Charlotte's flower shop is open seven days a week. (possessive noun)
5. I could feel the beat of the drums outside the club. (concrete noun)
6. University students sat on the library steps between classes. (plural noun)
7. On extremely hot days, the stench of garbage can be overwhelming. (concrete noun)
8. The city pulses with energy and excitement. (abstract noun)

Name _____ Date _____

 **Nouns**   *Application*

A. Supplying Nouns

Complete the paragraph by supplying nouns as indicated in parentheses. Write each word you would use on the blank line.

> Sydney is going to meet her friends at the *(1. proper noun)* this afternoon. Instead of walking, she decides to take the *(2. common noun)*. While getting ready to go, Sydney grabs her *(3. compound noun),* and notices that she still has her friend *(4. possessive proper noun)* CD. She liked the CD, and she admired the artists' *(5. abstract noun).* She plans to stop at the *(6. concrete noun)* and check out another CD by the same *(7. collective noun).*

1. _____   5. _____

2. _____   6. _____

3. _____   7. _____

4. _____

B. Writing with Nouns

Write sentences that contain the kinds of nouns indicated. Underline these nouns in your sentences.

1. Use a common noun and a plural noun.

_____

2. Use a proper noun and a collective noun.

_____

3. Use an abstract noun and a singular noun.

_____

4. Use a possessive noun and a proper noun.

_____

5. Use a compound noun and a concrete noun.

_____

6. Use a possessive noun and a common noun.

_____

7. Use an abstract noun and a plural noun.

_____

8. Use a concrete noun and a proper noun.

_____

Review 2 # Pronouns

Teaching

A **pronoun** is a word used in place of a noun or another pronoun.

Type of pronoun	Example	Function
personal	refers to first person, second person, and third person	I, you, he
possessive	shows ownership or belonging	mine, ours
reflexive	reflects an action back on a preceding noun or pronoun	himself
intensive	emphasizes a noun or pronoun in the same sentence	herself
interrogative	used to ask a question	who, what
demonstrative	points out specific persons, places, things, or ideas	that, those
relative	introduces a subordinate clause	who, which
indefinite	does not refer to a specific person or thing	someone

Finding Pronouns

Underline all the pronouns in the following sentences.

> **EXAMPLE** The distance <u>it</u> takes to stop <u>your</u> vehicle depends on several factors.

1. Many of the rules of driving involve simple common sense.
2. Patricia changed the flat tire herself.
3. What will they do if it breaks down on the highway?
4. He always stops to get a cold drink when he feels tired.
5. The state troopers themselves stay within the posted speed limit.
6. Moving at a fast speed means you will need more room between you and the car ahead of you.
7. Someone driving below the posted minimum speed poses a potential threat to others.
8. Use your low-beam headlights, not your brights, when driving in fog.
9. Keep your car safe by checking its oil and tire pressure often.
10. Which of the drivers at an intersection without a traffic control device has the right of way?
11. Yoshi prepared himself for the driving test.
12. Natasha blamed herself for not calling sooner to schedule her road test.
13. What should Daniel bring to the exam station?
14. Quiana stood in the line that seemed to move the slowest.
15. Jacqueline signed the card that permits donation of organs.
16. Our car horn was not in working order the day of the driving test.
17. My brother had mixed emotions about taking the driver's license exam.
18. You may help someone with your gift of a human organ.
19. Where do I sign this?
20. That is where you will have your picture taken.
21. My father himself drove me to the driving test.
22. Anyone who drives a car accepts great responsibility.

Review 2 Pronouns

A. Finding Pronouns

Underline the pronoun or pronouns described in parentheses after each sentence.

1. Laura admitted she was nervous before her driving test. (possessive)

2. My grandfather claims that he taught himself how to drive. (reflexive)

3. Both of my sisters have their driver's licenses. (indefinite)

4. The examiner told me to park the car, and then he got out. (personal)

5. I myself passed the test on my first try. (intensive)

6. What can I do to improve my driving? (interrogative)

7. Those are the same officers with whom I spoke at the bureau. (demonstrative)

8. Anyone who has taken driving lessons should be able to pass the test. (indefinite)

9. Can I drive you anywhere? (personal)

10. Are you the person to whom I should report? (relative)

11. Did somebody drop his or her car keys? (indefinite)

12. Sharese told herself to relax before her test. (reflexive)

13. Most of the drivers who have taken lessons pass the test on their first try. (indefinite)

14. The license itself confers on its owner both privileges and responsibilities. (intensive)

15. We are relieved that this day is over. (personal)

B. Identifying Pronouns

Underline the pronoun in each sentence and identify it by writing **personal, possessive, reflexive, intensive, interrogative, demonstrative, relative,** or **indefinite** on the line.

1. What are the requirements for obtaining a driver license? _____

2. Josh received his temporary license by passing two tests. _____

3. The manager of the driving school himself rode with Pat. _____

4. You have to study and learn all the material in the vehicle law book. _____

5. Our state requires drivers to pass a written test and a road test. _____

6. The examiner who administered Al's test carried a clipboard. _____

7. Is that the marker Halle's front bumper hit? _____

8. Which of the sections did Elijah pass, driving or maneuverability? _____

9. Everyone took lessons through the school's program. _____

10. Maeve drove herself to school the next day. _____

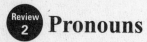

Pronouns

Application

A. Writing Sentences with Pronouns

Write sentences using the types of pronouns indicated. Underline the required pronouns in your sentences. Be sure the pronoun matches the person, number, and gender of its antecedent.

1. personal pronoun in the third person, nominative case

_____

2. personal pronoun in the first person, objective case

_____

3. possessive pronoun that stands alone

_____

4. demonstrative pronoun

_____

5. feminine reflexive pronoun

_____

B. Writing Dialogue with Pronouns

Underline all the pronouns in the dialogue below. Then write one more quotation from each of the two speakers. Include at least four of these kinds of pronouns: personal, possessive, demonstrative, reflexive, intensive, interrogative, indefinite, and relative. Underline the pronouns in your dialogue. Use a separate piece of paper if necessary.

"I can't believe this happened. My parents are going to be really upset. Look at their car! It is messed up! What will I tell them?"

"Just tell them the truth. They'll understand. I'm sure they'll just be glad we are all right."

"That is probably true. Even my Dad himself got into a fender bender last summer."

"See? He'll understand."

"Oh, what was I doing? I don't remember what I was thinking about when it happened. I guess I won't be driving everyone out to the farm next month. I am sure my parents will take away my car privileges."

_____

_____

_____

Verbs

Teaching

A **verb** is a word used to express an action, a condition, or a state of being.

An **action verb** expresses a physical or mental action. Action verbs may be transitive or intransitive. A **transitive verb** transfers the action from the subject toward a direct object. An **intransitive verb** does not transfer action so it does not have an object.

| **Transitive verb** | The lion <u>stalked</u> the antelope. (*Antelope* is the direct object.) |
| **Intransitive verb** | The antelope <u>ran</u> away. |

A **linking verb** connects the subject with a word or words that identify or describe the subject. Some linking verbs are forms of *be*, such as *am, is, was*, and *were*. Others express condition, such as *appear, become, feel, look, remain, sound*, and *taste*.

> The zebras <u>looked</u> startled.

An **auxiliary verb**, also called a **helping verb**, helps the main verb express action or make a statement. A **verb phrase** is made up of a main verb and one or more helping verbs. Some common auxiliary verbs are *had, do, might, will, must, could*, and *would*.

> The elephant <u>should be</u> <u>running</u> from the hunters. (The main verb is *running*.)

A. Identifying Verbs

Underline the verb or verb phrase in each sentence. In the space above each verb, write **A** if it is an action verb, **L** if it is a linking verb, or **AUX** if it is an auxiliary verb.

1. The passengers grew restless during the long train ride.

2. The colors of the fabrics seemed iridescent in the bright light.

3. An incorrect ZIP code might have delayed the letter.

4. Diego Rivera painted many significant murals in Mexico and the United States.

5. Have you measured the temperature of the water?

6. At the bottom of Carlsbad Caverns, the air feels cold and damp.

B. Identifying Transitive and Intransitive Verbs

Underline the verb or verb phrase in each sentence. On the line, write **T** for a transitive verb or **I** for an intransitive verb.

1. At the break of day, the lion stretched lazily. _____

2. It gazed at the grass-filled veldt around it. _____

3. Some animal movement in the distance caught its eye. _____

4. The gazelle herd was feeding fearlessly in the grass, unaware of the danger nearby. _____

5. The lion chose a small gazelle from the herd as its prey. _____

Review 3 Verbs

More Practice

A. Identifying Verbs

Underline each verb once. If the verb has a direct object, underline the direct object twice. In the space above each verb, write **T** for transitive or **I** for intransitive.

1. P. T. Barnum, the circus king, brought famous performers to America.

2. Opera stars, acrobats, animal trainers, and clowns performed in his circus.

3. Jenny Lind, "The Swedish Nightingale," joined about 1850.

4. The prima donna was then considering complete retirement.

5. Financial problems had troubled her for some time.

6. Both Lind and Barnum felt, at the time, fortunate with their deal.

7. An advance of $187,500 sealed the huge contract.

8. Barnum used many advertising and publicity stunts.

B. Using Verbs

Refer to the passage below to complete these items.

> The rhinoceros is a huge, heavy animal. It has thick skin and very little hair. Its magnificent horn grows throughout its lifetime. Although useful in battle, the rhinoceros's horn has become the source of its troubles in recent decades. Many hunters kill rhinos simply for their horns. They sell the horns, in a powdered form, all over the world. Today, wild rhinoceros live in Africa and in Southeast Asia. Another species of rhinoceros, the Sumatran rhinoceros, is now almost extinct. Aware of the constant threat of extinction, many countries and international organizations are now forbidding the hunting of the rhinoceros.

1. Find examples of two transitive verbs in the passage. On the lines below, write those verbs and the direct objects that receive their actions.

   Transitive verb 1: _____ Direct object: _____

   Transitive verb 2: _____ Direct object: _____

2. Write three action verbs from the passage on the lines below.

   _____ _____ _____

3. Write two verb phrases from the passage. Underline the auxiliary verbs in each phrase.

   _____ _____

4. Write one of the sentences from the passage that contains a linking verb. Underline the two words that are connected by the linking verb.

   _____

5. Find examples of two intransitive verbs in the passage. Write them on the lines below.

   _____ _____

Verbs

A. Writing with Verbs That Can Be Either Transitive or Intransitive

Underline the verb in each sentence. Write **T** above it if it is transitive or **I** if it is intransitive. Then, if it is transitive, use it as an intransitive verb in a sentence of your own. If it is intransitive, use it as a transitive verb. Write your new sentence on the line.

> **EXAMPLE** The bird <u>sang</u> outside my window. *The bird sang a sweet song.*

1. The photographers packed their equipment for the safari.

   _____

2. They had planned the trip for months.

   _____

3. The group gathered just before sunrise.

   _____

4. Their expert guides had walked the route many times before.

   _____

5. One participant forgot some of her film at base camp.

   _____

B. Proofreading

The writer of this paragraph was careless and omitted many verbs. Proofread the paragraph, looking for places where an action verb, a linking verb, or an auxiliary verb would improve the writing. Then insert this proofreading symbol ∧ and write the verb you wish to add above it.

> **EXAMPLE** Elephants ∧*are* the largest animals that live on land.

The great size of elephants is, in fact, their best protection. They have little fear of most animals, because they able to crush and kill small attackers. However, they do have powerful enemies, namely lions, crocodiles, snakes, and human beings. Adult elephants not usually attacked, but tigers and leopards killed elephant calves. Despite its size, the elephant can be gentle and tame. People trained elephants for thousands of years. Loggers elephants to carry heavy loads.

Most elephants in herds. They enjoy water and frequently swim in lakes and rivers. They grass, leaves, and bark, and they drink up to 40 gallons of water daily. Humans, the elephant's most dangerous enemy, destroyed much of its natural habitat, but today many African and Asian countries set aside land to protect elephants.

Adjectives and Adverbs

Teaching

Adjectives and adverbs are modifiers that describe other words in a sentence.

Adjectives modify nouns or pronouns. They qualify or specify the meaning of the words they modify. Adjectives answer the following questions: *What kind? Which one? How many? How much?*

<u>plastic</u> cup   <u>that</u> sign   <u>several</u> tables   <u>some</u> help

Predicate adjectives follow linking verbs and modify the subject of a sentence.

Pizza is <u>delicious</u>.   The warm bread smells <u>wonderful</u>.

Adverbs modify verbs, adjectives, or other adverbs. They answer the following questions about the words they modify: *how* (quickly, brightly); *where* (here, there, up); *when* (now, yesterday); and *to what extent* (very, too).

Finding Adjectives and Adverbs

Underline all the adjectives once in the following sentences, ignoring the articles. Underline the adverbs twice.

1. The wide variety of foods we eat every day links us to people everywhere.
2. The number of international foods you eat may surprise you.
3. Let us carefully examine some foods that one family eats.
4. Mrs. Jones eagerly drinks her first large cup of coffee early in the morning.
5. Coffee probably first came from the African country of Ethiopia, and it still grows there.
6. Mr. Jones usually prefers to drink a cup of hot tea.
7. British traders brought tea from China to thirsty people in Great Britain and in European countries.
8. It became a very popular hot beverage among the British.
9. The British brought their favorite drink to the American colonies in the 1700s.
10. The Jones children always have nutritious oatmeal.
11. Hot oatmeal has long been a breakfast tradition in the British Isles.
12. Mrs. Jones chooses some creamy yogurt for her morning snack.
13. This food originated in eastern Europe or central Asia.
14. After playing in the snow, the cold children want their cocoa.
15. Aztec Indians of Mexico enjoyed this rich beverage before Spanish explorers arrived in the Americas.
16. The whole family enthusiastically enjoys juicy hamburgers.
17. The popular hamburger originated as a meat patty in the German city of Hamburg.
18. Tonight the Jones family is eating rice, a food grain from Asia, as a side dish.
19. Mr. Jones never skips his snack of tasty corn chips.
20. These corn chips have recently been adapted from the traditional fried corn tortillas of the Mexican and Central American peoples.
21. These foods, and so many others, make the American diet truly multicultural.

Name _____ Date _____

Adjectives and Adverbs

More Practice

A. Identifying Adjectives

Underline each adjective once and underline the word it modifies twice. Some words are modified by more than one adjective. Do not underline articles.

1. Bread has been a basic food for most people for thousands of years.

2. White bread is quite popular in this country.

3. The French people love their crusty French bread, thin pancakes called crepes, and soft croissants.

4. Quick breads include tasty muffins and corn bread.

5. These breads have a crumbly texture, but can be made in a short time.

6. In some parts of the world, people eat thin, crisp sheets of flat bread.

7. Central American peoples eat various kinds of flat bread called tortillas.

8. These breads are made from corn meal.

9. People in eastern Asia make their flat bread from rice flour.

10. Obviously, bread is one food that can be found in many parts of the world in different forms.

B. Identifying Adverbs

Underline the word the boldfaced adverb modifies. If the word it modifies is a verb, write **V,** an adjective, write **ADJ,** or an adverb, write **ADV.**

1. Our library **seldom** allows renewal of books on the best-seller list.   _____

2. For his age and size, Max is an **unusually** fine running back.   _____

3. Today's assignment on dialects will be **thoroughly** discussed on Friday.   _____

4. You have made that point **before,** I believe.   _____

5. **Extremely** intense concentration is needed for a good game of chess.   _____

6. Two eaglets perched **somewhat** hesitantly at the edge of their treetop nest.   _____

7. George is **too** critical to enjoy working on a committee.   _____

8. Technology and federal subsidies have **radically** changed farming methods.   _____

9. During the puppet program, the toddlers behaved **quite** well.   _____

10. Too **quickly,** summer's days shortened into those of fall.   _____

Name _____ Date _____

Adjectives and Adverbs

Application

A. Writing Sentences with Adjectives and Adverbs

Revise each of these plain sentences by adding at least one adjective and one adverb. You may also add phrases if you wish. Write your new sentences on the lines below. Underline the adjectives once and the adverbs twice.

EXAMPLE Ally walked to the mall.
With two of her best friends, Ally walked slowly to the local mall.

1. The chef prepared a meal.

_____

2. The dinner guests took their places.

_____

3. The host offered a toast.

_____

4. The guests made conversation.

_____

5. The dinner party was a success!

_____

B. Writing with Adjectives and Adverbs

Playwrights often include directions to the actors about how to say their lines, how to hold their bodies, and where to move. Complete the stage directions below with adjectives or adverbs. Write your stage directions in the parentheses after each character's name.

Andy (speaking _____ and holding his stomach) I am so hungry!

Cal (in a _____ manner) So am I. I'm glad Coach Warren offered to bring back some lunch for us.

Dennis (_____ looking _____) I just hope he does not bring pizza. I am tired of pizza.

Andy (_____ and with a _____ expression) Especially pizza with anchovies!

Cal (_____ and in a _____ voice) I would really prefer some carrot sticks and veggie burgers for a change.

Darryl (_____ from across the field) And some fruit juice!

Coach Warren (_____ moving _____ to the boys) I'm back! I know teenagers love pizza, and since you guys will eat anything, I got it with anchovies! And plenty of soft drinks for all!

Cal and Andy (_____ and turning their heads away) Yuck!
(_____ and trying to hide their feelings) Great! Let's eat!

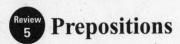

Review 5 **Prepositions**   *Teaching*

A **preposition** is a word used to show the relationship between a noun or pronoun and some other word in the sentence. A preposition always introduces a phrase called a **prepositional phrase.** A prepositional phrase ends in a noun or a pronoun called an **object of the preposition.** Any modifiers of the object are also part of the prepositional phrase.

> Hang the large painting **on the far wall.** (The preposition is *on,* the object of the preposition is *wall,* and the prepositional phrase is *on the far wall.*)

A **compound preposition** is a preposition that consists of more than one word. Some examples of compound prepositions include the following: *according to, in addition to, aside from, in place of,* and *by means of.* **Compound objects** are two or more objects of a single proposition.

> The museum displays sculptures <u>in addition to</u> <u>paintings</u> and <u>tapestries</u>.
>   COMPOUND   COMPOUND OBJECTS
>   PREPOSITION

Finding Prepositions

Underline each preposition once. Remember that compound prepositions have two or more words. Underline each object of the preposition twice.

1. You can visit traditional museums like art museums or planetariums.
2. If you prefer, you can travel across the country seeing unusual museums.
3. You might choose the Banana Museum in California.
4. Within its walls is a great banana article collection.
5. If you want a banana cookie jar, banana magnets, or books about bananas, the Banana Museum is your place.
6. The Toaster Museum has an impressive collection showing the toaster's impact on popular culture.
7. Unfortunately, the Toaster Museum is presently without a permanent home.
8. Are you a magic fan? Visit the Houdini Historical Center, a museum devoted to the great magician Harry Houdini.
9. The center contains lock picks, handcuffs, and straitjackets used by Houdini.
10. Why not visit one of Florida's stranger museums, the Teddy Bear Museum?
11. Its teddy bear collection numbers over 2,300 furry friends.
12. You might enjoy stepping into the Shoe Museum.
13. A recent addition includes jogging shoes from Bill Clinton.
14. In New Mexico, see the American International Rattlesnake Museum.
15. You might like Max Nordeen's Wheel Museum because of its spark plug collection and vintage cars.
16. See the Hamburger Museum and enjoy standing beside a hamburger waterbed and a hamburger motorcycle.
17. If you are Texas-bound, see the Cockroach Hall of Fame.
18. In spite of its name, the museum has some interesting exhibits.

Prepositions

More Practice

A. Identifying Prepositions

Underline each preposition once. Underline each object of the preposition twice.
A sentence may have more than one prepositional phrase.

1. Many clocks are powered by a mainspring.
2. Neither candidate avoided controversy during the presidential debate.
3. After lunch Paul washed the dishes and finished his chores.
4. At the bird feeder, Denise identified three species of sparrows.
5. Out of a thicket a brace of partridges flew.
6. There are many legends about Johnny Appleseed.
7. According to today's newspaper, a local factory is closing.
8. He carefully placed the extra key inside the brown vase beside the oak bookcase.
9. Searchers found the box beneath fallen rafters.
10. Let's shoot some baskets after school and before dinner.

B. Writing with Prepositional Phrases

Underline the prepositional phrase in each sentence. Then replace that phrase and
write your new sentence on the line. Be sure to use a different preposition and a
new object of the preposition.

EXAMPLE We took a tour <u>through the museum's new exhibit</u>.
We took a tour with a guide.

1. We visited the Natural History Museum instead of the Art Museum.

   _____

2. Standing beside actual dinosaur bones was a big thrill.

   _____

3. We liked every exhibit except the insect exhibit.

   _____

4. We saw the shell collection in addition to the butterfly collection.

   _____

5. The museum is famous on account of its huge dioramas.

   _____

6. I bought a book about our state's geology.

   _____

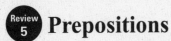

Prepositions

Application

A. Writing with Prepositional Phrases

Add one or more prepositional phrases to each simple sentence. Write your new sentence on the line.

1. The family waited for the bus.

_____

2. They got off the bus.

_____

3. Excitedly, they walked.

_____

4. The museum guard welcomed them.

_____

5. They saw paintings.

_____

6. They left the museum.

_____

B. Writing with Prepositional Phrases

Use six of these prepositional phrases in an original story. Write your story on the lines below. Use a separate piece of paper if necessary.

above the front door	beside his signature	away from the guard
under a giant chandelier	against the far wall	among the visitors
after the tour	without any doubt	in the gift shop

_____

_____

_____

_____

_____

_____

_____

_____

_____

Review 6

Conjunctions and Interjections

Teaching

A **conjunction** is a word used to join words or groups of words.

Type	Function
coordinating	connects words or word groups that have equal importance in a sentence *(and, but, or, for, so, yet, nor)*
correlative	pairs of conjunctions that connect words or groups of words *(both . . . and, either . . . or, not only . . . but also)*
subordinating	introduce subordinate clauses—clauses that cannot stand alone as complete sentences. Some common subordinating conjunctions include *after, because, before, in order that, since, until, when,* and *while.*

A **conjunctive adverb** is an adverb used as a coordinating conjunction. Examples include *finally, still, besides, however,* and *otherwise.*

An **interjection** is a word or short phrase used to express emotion, such as *wow* and *my goodness.*

Identifying Conjunctions and Interjections

In the following sentences, underline the conjunctions once and underline the conjunctive adverbs twice. Draw parentheses around any interjections. Remember that there are two parts to a correlative conjunction.

1. Wow! A strange object fell from the sky and crashed into Roswell, New Mexico.
2. Both photographers and reporters covered the story.
3. Honestly, before the object fell, few people had heard of Roswell.
4. No one knows what happened that day; nevertheless, many people find the incident fascinating.
5. People believed that a spaceship had landed, but the Air Force had a different explanation.
6. First the government confirmed the rumors, and then they denied them.
7. A scientist named Stanton Friedman was surprised by the eyewitness stories he heard; consequently, he wrote a book about the incident.
8. "Unbelievable! When I visited the crash site," one eyewitness claims, "I saw an alien craft."
9. Ridiculous! Neither Air Force investigators nor government spokespersons support that claim.
10. Some people believe that the government hid the evidence so that they could study the aliens in secret.
11. "The cover-up began then; moreover, it is still going on," the skeptics say.
12. Men guarding the site saw important details, yet they stayed silent.
13. As long as people enjoy a good mystery, the incident will not be forgotten.
14. Either the witnesses are mistaken or someone is hiding the truth.
15. The Roswell incident continues to puzzle and fascinate the public.

Review 6

Conjunctions and Interjections

More Practice

A. Identifying Conjunctions, Conjunctive Adverbs, and Interjections

In the following sentences, underline the conjunctions once and underline the conjunctive adverbs twice. Draw parentheses around any interjections.

1. An unidentified flying object, also called a UFO, is a strange light or object that appears in the sky.

2. Some people believe UFOs are spaceships from other planets, but there is no proof for this.

3. Observers insist UFOs are spaceships since they fly in erratic, unusual patterns.

4. Either people are making up these stories, or they are mistaking one thing for another.

5. After some witnesses reported a UFO sighting, the object was proven to be a weather balloon.

6. Some people believe that aliens have not only visited Earth, but they also have taken humans aboard their ships. Incredible!

7. Your response might be "Crazy!"; still, the Air Force has investigated over 12,000 UFO reports.

8. The Air Force undertook this project to determine whether the UFOs were a threat to national security or a persistent hoax.

9. The Air Force ended the project in 1969; finally, they stated with certainty that the country was under no threat from unidentified flying objects.

10. Some evening, when you are gazing at the sky, you may still want to keep a lookout for a UFO.

B. Using Conjunctions, Conjunctive Adverbs, and Interjections

Complete each of the following sentences with a conjunction, a conjunctive adverb, or an interjection.

EXAMPLE We put an ad in the newspaper, _____*yet*_____ nobody responded.

1. _____ this pair of leather shoes _____ that pair of suede boots would look fine.

2. Frank Lloyd Wright was known for both his commercial buildings _____ his homes.

3. "Dark horse" was originally a term for a promising _____ untried racehorse.

4. The dodo was a clumsy bird; _____, its wings were useless.

5. Whether Luther goes out _____ stays home, he has to do the dishes.

6. _____ the opera was unusually long, few people left before the end.

7. _____ trigonometry _____ calculus is an easy subject for me.

Review 6

Conjunctions and Interjections

Application

REVIEW

A. Choosing Conjunctions and Conjunctive Adverbs

Revise the following paragraph by adding conjunctions and conjunctive adverbs where they are needed. Choose from the list of words to the right.

Reports of small, glowing balls of light that not only move at high speed

_____ make complex maneuvers are not new. During World War II,

both Allied _____ German airmen spotted these glowing balls.

Pilots reported seeing balls of fire that appeared suddenly _____

lingered for miles. The Allies thought these balls were a German secret

weapon _____ the Germans assumed they were a new Allied

weapon. United States pilots called them "foo fighters"; _____ the

balls of light never attacked. _____ many people saw these foo

fighters, it was never determined exactly what they were.

**but also
and
while
but
however
although
until
so**

B. Writing a Diary Entry with Conjunctions and Interjections

Suppose you had seen the landing of a UFO piloted by alien beings. On the lines below, write a diary entry for that day. Use at least two coordinating conjunctions, two correlative conjunctions, two subordinating conjunctions, two conjunctive adverbs, and two interjections. Below your diary entry, list your conjunctions, conjunctive adverbs, and interjections under the appropriate headings.

_____

_____

_____

_____

_____

_____

_____

_____

Coordinating Conjunctions   **Correlative Conjunctions**   **Interjections**

_____   _____   _____

_____   _____   _____

Subordinating Conjunctions   **Conjunctive Adverbs**

_____   _____

_____   _____

Subjects and Predicates

Teaching

A **sentence** is a group of words that expresses a complete thought. Every sentence can be divided into two parts: the subject and the predicate. The most basic elements of a sentence are the simple subject and the simple predicate. The **simple subject** tells who or what performs the action in a sentence. The **simple predicate**, or **verb**, tells what the subject did or what happened to the subject.

> Storytellers kept the ancient legend alive for centuries.
> SIMPLE   SIMPLE
> SUBJECT   PREDICATE

The **complete subject** includes the simple subject and all the words that modify it. The **complete predicate** includes all the words that tell what the subject did or what happened to the subject.

> The war between the Greeks and the Trojans lasted for many years.
> COMPLETE SUBJECT   COMPLETE PREDICATE

A **sentence fragment** is a group of words that is only part of a sentence. It may lack a subject, a predicate, or both.

A. Identifying Subjects and Predicates

If the simple subject is boldfaced, write **SS** on the line. If the simple predicate is boldfaced, write **SP**. Write **CS** if the boldfaced words are the complete subject or **CP** if they are the complete predicate.

1. Seeds for the Trojan War **were sown at the wedding feast of Peleus.** _____

2. All the gods and goddesses **were invited** except for Eris, the goddess of discord. _____

3. The angry goddess **sent a golden apple inscribed "For the most beautiful."** _____

4. **Paris, who loved Helen,** settled the dispute of who was most beautiful. _____

5. Paris **awarded** the apple to the goddess Aphrodite, who had promised him Helen. _____

6. Helen **had been promised** to King Menelaus. _____

7. When Paris stole Helen, **Menelaus** became angry. _____

8. **Menelaus and his brother** assembled an army to fight Troy, Paris's home. _____

B. Identifying Complete Sentences

Read each of the following groups of words. If the words form a complete sentence, write **S** on the line. If the words form a sentence fragment, write **F** and tell if it is missing a subject **(MS)** or a predicate **(MP)**.

1. Retold the story of the epic battles for centuries. _____

2. The women warriors, the Amazons, fought for the Trojans. _____

3. The Greek warrior Achilles and his friend Patroclus. _____

4. Built a huge, hollow wooden horse and filled it with Greek soldiers. _____

5. The soldiers waiting inside the huge horse that was taken into Troy. _____

Lesson 1

Subjects and Predicates

More Practice

A. Identifying Subjects and Predicates

Draw a vertical line between the complete subject and the complete predicate.
Then underline the simple subject once and underline the simple predicate twice.

EXAMPLE The *Iliad* by the Greek poet Homer | <u>tells</u> the story of the Trojan War.

1. The poet describes various incidents in the final year of the long war.
2. The army of Greece eventually defeats the Trojans.
3. Brave heroes such as Achilles and Hector are featured in the poem.
4. The story of the *Iliad* covers a period of 54 days.
5. The poet focuses particularly on the events in the Greek camp.
6. Achilles, one of the greatest heroes of the Greeks, has withdrawn from the battle over a disagreement with his leaders.
7. The Trojans take advantage of the Greeks after Achilles' departure.
8. The Trojan warrior Hector kills Achilles' friend Patroclus.
9. An enraged Achilles seeks revenge against Hector.
10. The story of the *Iliad* ends with Hector's funeral in Troy.

B. Using Complete Subjects and Predicates

On the line to the right of each item, write how each of the following groups of
words could be used: **CS** for a complete subject or **CP** for a complete predicate.
Then use each group of words to write a complete sentence, adding a complete
subject or complete predicate as necessary.

EXAMPLE lost the game in the bottom of the ninth inning *CP*
This frustrating team lost the game in the bottom of the ninth inning.

1. some of the science projects _____

_____

2. swam to a small island in the middle of the river _____

_____

3. downhill skiers with years of experience _____

_____

4. tastes best cold _____

_____

5. hot buttered pancakes _____

_____

6. hung from the lowest branch of the tree _____

_____

CHAPTER 1

Lesson 1

Subjects and Predicates

Application

A. Writing Subjects and Predicates

Write sentences on the lines below by adding both a subject and a predicate to each fragment. Do not use the fragment as the subject of the sentence.

> EXAMPLE during the heat of battle
> *Many soldiers showed courage during the heat of battle.*

1. a long column of numbers

_____

2. her brother and sister

_____

3. the elements on the periodic table

_____

4. the editor of the school newspaper

_____

5. a bus schedule for the downtown area

_____

6. a wrench from the plumber's toolbox

_____

B. Adding Subjects and Predicates

Read this paragraph carefully. It contains several sentence fragments. When you find a sentence fragment, insert this proofreading symbol ∧ and write the words necessary to complete the sentence above the symbol.

> EXAMPLE The poet Homer ∧ the Odyssey.
> *wrote*

The poet Homer known not only for the epic poem the *Iliad* but also for the poem the *Odyssey*. Like the *Iliad,* the *Odyssey* deals with the Trojan War. However, in this poem the main is Odysseus, one of the heroes in the Greek army and the king of Ithaca. Odysseus a series of adventures on his way home from the historic battle. For example, encounters a one-eyed giant called Cyclops. The Cyclops captures Odysseus and his men, but they eventually escape by blinding the monster with a hot stake. Odysseus finally home. There meets noblemen trying to take over his kingdom. He defeats them in a contest of strength and skill and takes his rightful place on his throne.

CHAPTER 1

Lesson 2

Compound Sentence Parts

Teaching

A **compound subject** is made up of two or more subjects that share the same verb.

<u>Dogs</u> and <u>cats</u> often fight.

A **compound verb** is made up of two or more verbs or verb phrases that share the same subject.

Cats <u>hiss</u> and <u>scratch</u>.

A **compound predicate** includes a compound verb and all the words that go with each verb.

Sometimes cats <u>arch their backs</u> and <u>puff out their fur</u>.

Conjunctions join compound sentence parts and make the relationship between the parts clear. For example, *and* shows a combination, *or* or *either . . . or* shows a choice, and *neither . . . nor* shows a negative choice.

Identifying Simple Subjects and Verbs

In each sentence, underline the simple subject(s) once and the verb(s) twice. Write **CS** if the sentence has a compound subject or **CV** if it has a compound verb. The sentences with compound predicates have already been identified.

EXAMPLE <u>Veterinarians</u> <u>diagnose</u> and <u>treat</u> illnesses in animals. *CV*

1. Dogs and cats visit vets regularly for checkups and shots. _____

2. After all, rabies and tuberculosis may be transmitted to humans from animals. _____

3. Vets check animals for disease and teach their owners effective pet care. *CP*

4. Neither house pets nor farm animals stay perfectly healthy all their lives. _____

5. Vets understand the needs of farmers and fight widespread outbreaks of disease. *CP*

6. Either injuries or disease is the cause of most visits to vets. _____

7. On office visits, healthy pets undergo and benefit from thorough checkups. _____

8. Vets diagnose and medicate diseased animals. _____

9. Farm vets test dairy cattle for disease and often prescribe antibiotics. *CP*

10. Graduates of four-year veterinary college first receive their licenses and then make decisions about where to work. *CP*

11. Either private practice or research may be the choice of the graduating vet. _____

12. The U.S. Public Health Service and the U.S. Department of Agriculture employ some research-oriented vets. _____

13. Animal owners trust and respect veterinarians. _____

Lesson 2

Compound Sentence Parts

More Practice

A. Identifying Compound Sentence Parts

All of these sentences have either a compound subject, a compound verb, or a compound predicate. In every sentence, underline simple subject(s) once and the verb(s) twice.

> **EXAMPLE** Many talented <u>singers</u> and <u>dancers</u> <u>work</u> long hours.

1. Careers in entertainment attract a large number of people but are notoriously elusive.
2. Many actors and singers enjoy the excitement of stage acting or live TV shows.
3. Some actors either perform in films or find parts in television shows.
4. Neither long hours of practice nor high hopes guarantee success.
5. Luck is unpredictable and often plays a huge part in an actor's career.

B. Using Compound Subjects, Compound Verbs, and Compound Predicates

Combine the sentence pairs to form a new sentence with the sentence part indicated in parentheses. Use the conjunction *(either . . . or; neither . . . nor; and, or, nor, or but)* that makes the most sense.

> **EXAMPLE** Bicycles are environment-friendly alternatives to cars. In-line skates are also alternatives. (compound subject)
> *Bicycles and in-line skates are environment-friendly alternatives to cars.*

1. Jill cleaned the old silverware. She polished it too. (compound verb)

_____

2. The audience applauded for the world-famous pianist. Then they cheered for her. (compound verb)

_____

3. The volunteers sandbagged the river. They could not prevent the floodwaters from overflowing the banks. (compound predicate)

_____

4. The legends did not keep Peter from staying the night in the old house. The newspaper reports, also, did not have any effect on him. (compound subject)

_____

5. Brandy loves winter and participates in as many winter sports as she can. Her father is the same. (compound subject and compound predicate)

_____

6. Greg will paint the props. Perhaps Diane will paint them. (compound subject)

_____

CHAPTER 1

Lesson 2

Compound Sentence Parts   *Application*

A. Sentence Combining with Compound Subjects, Compound Verbs, and Compound Predicates

Combine each pair of sentences by writing a compound subject, a compound verb, or a compound predicate. Be sure that the subject and the verb agree in number.

1. Construction workers build houses, factories, and other buildings. They also repair these buildings.

_____

2. Architects are highly skilled construction workers. Civil engineers are also highly skilled workers.

_____

3. Carpenters construct the frameworks of buildings. They also hang doors and windows.

_____

4. Plumbers often train at vocational schools. Electricians also may train at vocational schools.

_____

5. General contractors estimate building costs. They supervise construction work.

_____

B. More Sentence Combining

Revise the following paragraph using compound subjects, compound verbs, and compound predicates to combine sentences with similar ideas. Write the new paragraph on the lines below. Use a separate piece of paper if necessary.

  Environmentalists are people who protect the environment. They also improve the environment. They can work indoors in classrooms, laboratories, or offices. They can work outdoors in forests, shorelines, or cities. Environmentalists preserve wildlife. They develop recreational areas. Farmers go to these specialists for advice. City planners ask their advice, also. Society has become more concerned about the environment. It will require the expertise of environmentalists even more in the future.

_____

_____

_____

_____

_____

Lesson 3

Subjects in Sentences

Teaching

There are four types of sentences, each with a specific function. In most sentences, the subject comes before the verb. A **declarative sentence** states a fact, a wish, an intent, or a feeling. An **interrogative sentence** asks a question. An **imperative sentence** gives a command, a request, or a direction. The subject of an imperative sentence is *you,* and it is usually understood, not stated. An **exclamatory sentence** expresses strong feeling.

Declarative	Abigail Becker lived on Long Point on Lake Erie.
Interrogative	Can the average person become a hero?
Imperative	Stay in port when bad weather is predicted.
Exclamatory	How brave Abigail was that night!

In an **inverted sentence,** the subject appears after the verb or between the words that make up the verb phrase. An inverted sentence can be used for variety or emphasis. Inverted word order is used in most interrogative sentences, to change the emphasis in declarative or exclamatory sentences, and in sentences beginning with *here* or *there.*

How <u>could</u> the <u>sailors</u> <u>survive</u>? (The subject interrupts the verb phrase *could survive.*)

Into the wild lake <u>swam</u> <u>Abigail</u>.
VERB SUBJECT

Here <u>was</u> a brave <u>woman</u>.
VERB   SUBJECT

Identifying Kinds of Sentences

On the line to the right of each sentence, identify the sentence as **DEC** for declarative, **INT** for interrogative, **IMP** for imperative, or **EXC** for exclamatory. Add the proper punctuation mark at the end of each sentence: question mark for interrogative, exclamation point for exclamatory or emotional imperative, and period for all others.

1. Bad weather struck the schooner *Conductor* on Lake Erie in November 1984 _____

2. Could the captain avoid the hidden sandbars and return to port safely _____

3. Swim for shore or you will die _____

4. How cold the water was _____

5. Abigail Becker swam to the crew members and pulled them back to shore _____

6. Thank the quiet young woman who saved your life _____

B. Finding Subjects and Verbs in Sentences

In the following sentences, underline each simple subject once and each verb or verb phrase twice. If the subject is understood, write *You* in parentheses on the line.

1. Within each gene is information about a hereditary trait. _____

2. Why do we shiver in cold weather? _____

3. Stop at the third intersection after the traffic signal. _____

Lesson 3 **Subjects in Sentences** *More Practice*

Using Different Kinds of Sentences

On the line to the right of each sentence, identify each sentence as **DEC** for declarative, **INT** for interrogative, **IMP** for imperative, or **EXC** for exclamatory. Add the correct end punctuation to each of these sentences. Then rewrite the sentences according to the instructions in parentheses. Use the same subject and verb. You may have to add or delete words and change word order.

> **EXAMPLE** The sunshine certainly feels good on my back *Dec*
> (Change to an interrogative sentence.)
> *Does the sunshine feel good on your back?*

1. Did you hear the weather forecast for today   _____
(Change to a declarative sentence.)

_____

2. Set your alarm for 6 o'clock sharp   _____
(Change to an interrogative sentence.)

_____

3. Did you notice the symmetry in this painting   _____
(Change to an imperative sentence.)

_____

4. That sound could be the fire alarm   _____
(Change to an exclamatory sentence.)

_____

B. Writing Sentences

Rewrite each sentence to make the verb come before the subject. You may rewrite it as a question or an inverted sentence, or you may begin the sentence with *here* or *there.* Then underline each subject once and underline each verb twice in your new sentence.

> **EXAMPLE** The manta ray swam over the ocean floor.
> *Over the ocean floor* <u>*swam*</u> *the* <u>*manta ray*</u>*.*

1. The coral reefs are there.

_____

2. The brave rescuer waded into the surf.

_____

3. A week's supply of newspapers is piled up by your front door.

_____

Lesson 3

Subjects in Sentences

Application

A. Revising Using a Variety of Sentence Types

The writer of this paragraph decided to use only declarative sentences with the traditional word order of subject before verb. Rewrite the paragraph, this time using a variety of sentence types.

> Terry Fox was 18 years old and a college student in Vancouver, Canada, when he learned he had bone cancer. His dreams of becoming a professional athlete were shattered by this discovery. Terry's right leg was amputated above the knee. However, Terry refused to give up sports. He decided to run across Canada to raise money for cancer research. Terry's journey began on April 12, 1980. He started running on the Atlantic coast in Newfoundland and planned on running all the way to the Pacific Ocean. Unfortunately, his cancer spread more quickly than anticipated, and Terry died before reaching his goal. Nevertheless, other cancer victims gained hope from his strength.

_____

_____

_____

_____

_____

B. Revising Using a Variety of Sentence Orders

The writer of this paragraph decided to use both traditional word order of subject before verb and a less traditional inverted sentence order. Rewrite the paragraph, this time using a variety of sentence orders to make it more understandable and pleasing to the reader.

> Do I have dreams of foreign travel? Definitely. Here is my current wish. I would love to see Paris. What do I admire about Paris? Filled with so much history is that magnificent city. Beautiful are its many gardens and parks. So excited would I be to see the Eiffel Tower! Visiting the Louvre Museum would be one of the first things I would do when I arrived. There are outdoor cafés to enjoy and churches to visit. However, here is the problem—enough money for such a trip have I not. So, for now, my dream will be just that—a dream.

_____

_____

_____

_____

_____

CHAPTER 1

Lesson 4

Complements

Teaching

Complements are words or groups of words that complete the meaning or action of verbs. A **direct object** is a noun or pronoun that tells who or what receives the action of a verb. A sentence with an direct object may also have an **indirect object,** a noun or pronoun that tells *to* or *for whom* or *what* the action of the verb is done. (An indirect object never follows a preposition.)

Direct object	Marco Polo told <u>stories</u> of faraway Cathay.
Indirect object	He told his <u>readers</u> stories of his travels.

An **objective complement** is a noun or adjective that follows the direct object and identifies or describes it. Only a few verbs and their synonyms can be followed by objective complements, including *appoint, call, choose, consider, elect, find, keep, make, name,* and *think.*

Objective complement	Some historians consider Polo's tales <u>unreliable</u>.

Subject complements are words that follow linking verbs and identify and describe the subjects. **Predicate nominatives** are nouns or pronouns that function as subject complements. **Predicate adjectives** are adjectives that function as subject complements.

Predicate nominative	Marco Polo's journey was a historical <u>wonder</u>.
Predicate adjective	His tales were almost <u>unbelievable</u>.

Identifying Linking Verbs and Subject Complements

On each line, identify the boldfaced word as a direct object **(DO)**, an indirect object **(IO)**, an objective complement **(OC)**, a predicate nominative **(PN)**, or a predicate adjective **(PA).**

1. Marco Polo was an Italian **trader** during the 13th and 14th centuries.   _____

2. He is **famous** for his remarkable stories of travels in China at a time when China was a distant mystery.   _____

3. In 1269, Marco's father and uncle brought back **tales** of their adventures in the Far East.   _____

4. Their stories inspired **Marco** and made him long to visit China himself, and his wish was granted only two years later.   _____

5. Marco took detailed **notes** about what he saw along the way.   _____

6. The great Mongol leader Kublai Khan considered the Polo family his **friends** for years.   _____

7. He gave **them** gifts of jewels, silk, and ivory.   _____

8. He also gave the **Polo family** orders to stay in China; however, fearing for their lives, they eventually escaped.   _____

9. Twenty-four years after starting their journey, the Polo family told their **neighbors** in Venice exciting stories about the East.   _____

10. Some people, then and now, consider the stories **untrue.**   _____

Lesson 4

Complements

More Practice

A. Identifying Complements

In each of the following sentences, underline the complement indicated in parentheses.

> **EXAMPLE** Hong Kong is <u>one</u> of the busiest ports in the world.
> (predicate nominative)

1. Great Britain long considered Hong Kong a colony. (objective complement)
2. Hong Kong is now a special administrative region of China. (predicate nominative)
3. Great Britain told the people of Hong Kong that they would relinquish control of Hong Kong after 99 years. (indirect object)
4. No matter who controls this region, it is clearly prosperous. (predicate adjective)
5. Hong Kong is home to more than 6.5 million people. (predicate nominative)
6. Hong Kong even has its own flag, which features a red background with a white, five-petaled flower in the center. (direct object)
7. Hong Kong offers the world textiles as well as sophisticated electronic equipment. (indirect object)
8. The fact that Hong Kong collected no import duties on imported goods made it a base of operations for many international businesses. (objective complement)
9. Because it has so many residents and so little vacant land, Hong Kong is always anxious to import large amounts of foods. (predicate adjective)
10. Many workers ride the ferry from Kowloon to Hong Kong every day. (direct object)

B. Using Subject Complements

Complete each sentence below. First complete it with a predicate nominative. Then complete it with a predicate adjective.

> **EXAMPLE** The old house was *a colonial*.
> The old house was *empty*.

1. The architect was _____.

   The architect was _____.

2. The last owner was _____.

   The last owner was _____.

3. The garden became _____.

   The garden became _____.

4. The neighborhood is _____.

   The neighborhood is _____.

5. The old house will someday be _____.

   The old house will someday be _____.

Lesson 4

Complements

Application

A. Using Complements in Sentences

Choose one group of words from each list below to complete each sentence. Use each item only once. Each sentence should have both an indirect object and a direct object. If you wish, you can add words to make the sentences more interesting.

Indirect objects	Direct objects
her friends	a birthday cake
the new players	a thank-you note
the parakeet	flowers
his wife	her new watch
the hostess	a few pointers
their families	two new words
the customers	their dinners
her daughter	postcards

1. Misty showed _____.

2. Mr. Stuart sent _____.

3. The tennis pro gave _____.

4. Mrs. Davis baked _____.

5. A considerate guest writes _____.

6. The tourists sent _____.

7. The trainer taught _____.

8. The waiter served _____.

B. Writing Subject Complements

Complete each sentence in the following passage with either a predicate nominative or a predicate adjective. Following your sentence, write **PN** if you have used a predicate nominative or **PA** if you have used a predicate adjective.

(1) Traveling to a foreign country can be _____. **(2)** Seeing new sights is _____. **(3)** However, trying to find your way in a new place is often _____. **(4)** Not understanding the language may be _____. **(5)** When you want to take a bus, train, or plane, the experience is sometimes _____.

1. _____

2. _____

3. _____

4. _____

5. _____

Lesson 5

Sentence Diagramming

More Practice 1

Complete each diagram with the sentence provided.

A. Simple Subjects and Simple Predicates

Cities grow.

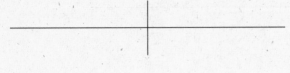

Los Angeles has grown.

B. Compound Subjects, Compound Verbs, and Modifiers

Compound Subject

Homes and businesses are built.

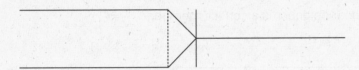

Compound Verb

New residents move in and settle down.

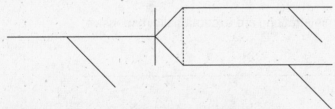

C. Direct Objects and Indirect Objects

Direct Object Cities quickly establish governments.

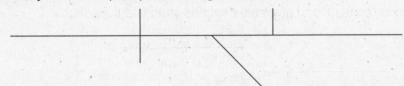

Indirect Object Efficient city governments give residents the necessary services.

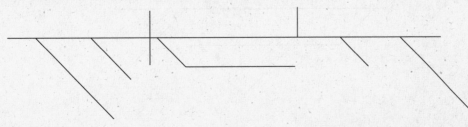

Sentence Diagramming

Lesson 5

More Practice 2

D. Objective Complements

Unsafe streets made citizens upset.

The mayor appointed a police officer commissioner.

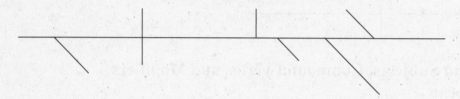

E. Subject Complements

Predicate Nominative My next-door neighbor is a council member.

Predicate Adjective Some city administrations are exceptionally responsive.

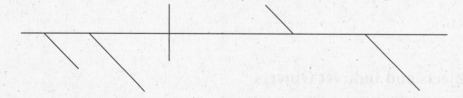

Our mayor is honest and competent, and gives his deputies adequate support.

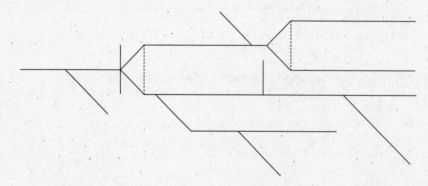

Sentence Diagramming

Application

On a separate piece of paper, diagram each of the following sentences.

A. Diagramming Subjects, Verbs, Objects, and Modifiers

1. Several work crews clean highways and residential streets constantly.

2. Police officers and detectives investigate crimes.

3. Firefighters answer alarms immediately.

4. Many cities give senior citizens special services.

B. Diagramming Objective Complements and Subject Complements

1. Some maintenance jobs look difficult.

2. That tree trimmer calls his job exciting.

3. Snow makes winter traffic a headache.

4. Many Southern cities regard rain their biggest problem.

C. Mixed Practice

1. Mayor Black appointed Captain Davis his new safety director.

2. Newspaper reporters and television crews attended the news conference.

3. The mayor gave one station an exclusive interview.

4. Director Davis's immediate concern is juvenile crime.

5. A water main burst nearby and stopped traffic.

6. Some residents called their street lights a disgrace.

7. Yesterday, numerous home owners and concerned renters staged a protest.

8. A mayoral candidate needs self-confidence, energy, and good humor.

Prepositional Phrases

Teaching

A **prepositional phrase** consists of a preposition, its object, and any modifiers of the object.

> The name, Helen, means "light" <u>in Greek</u>. (The preposition is *in*.)
> Children <u>in India, Africa, and Israel</u> usually have names <u>with a specific meaning</u>.

An **adjective phrase** is a prepositional phrase that acts as an adjective to modify a noun or a pronoun. It tells *what kind* or *which one*.

> Many <u>of the common given names</u> are from Latin. (The phrase modifies *many*, explaining of what.)

An **adverb phrase** is a prepositional phrase that modifies a verb, an adjective, or another adverb. It usually tells *where, when, how,* or *to what extent*.

> <u>During their lifetime</u>, American Indians often use several different names. (The phrase modifies *use*, telling when.)

Usually, a prepositional phrase should be placed before or immediately after the word or words it modifies.

A. Identifying Prepositional Phrases

Underline every prepositional phrase in each sentence.

> **EXAMPLE** Personal names <u>for individuals</u> have been <u>in use since</u> <u>early human history</u>.

1. Names for families have been in use for centuries.
2. An emperor of China demanded the use of family names by the people in his land.
3. In Europe during the Middle Ages, titles were adopted by people of high rank.
4. After a while, even people without rank insisted on a family name.
5. Often the name for a family was based on the town, occupation, or nickname of the head of the family.
6. For example, names like *Miller, Cook,* and *Smith* came from jobs.
7. *Rockefeller* comes from a Dutch word with the original meaning of "dweller near a field of rye."
8. Naturally, Johnson started with the "son of John."

B. Identifying Words Modified by Prepositional Phrases

Underline the prepositional phrase once in each of the following sentences. Underline the word it modifies twice.

1. Willard ran toward the goal.
2. A flock of Canadian geese honked loudly outside.
3. Exotic animals from Australia and New Zealand were featured.
4. The girl on the left is my cousin, Phyllis.
5. The luxurious cruise ship dropped anchor in the bay.
6. Far overhead, the jet streaked through the darkening sky.
7. Jumbo ice cream sundaes with whipped cream satisfied us completely.
8. Smith Library is between the book store and the student center.

Prepositional Phrases

More Practice

A. Identifying Prepositional Phrases

In each sentence, underline twice the word modified by the underlined prepositional phrase. On the blank, write **ADJ** or **ADV** to identify what kind of prepositional phrase it is.

1. <u>During the Middle Ages</u>, natural surroundings gave many people their family names. _____

2. If you lived <u>near a hill</u> in England, you might get the name *Hill*. _____

3. A family <u>from France</u> who lived near a hill would get the name *Dumont*. _____

4. People called *Wood, Stone,* and *Brook* probably come <u>from families</u> that lived hear those natural features. _____

5. Most people <u>of the Middle Ages</u> could not read and, therefore, relied on pictures. _____

6. To identify their shops, shopkeepers hung up signs <u>with pictures</u>. _____

7. The picture on the sign might give a name <u>to the owner</u> of the shop. _____

8. If the sign <u>on your shop</u> showed a bell, you might become Mr. or Mrs. Bell. _____

9. Another common source of family names was the names <u>of towns</u>. _____

10. Most English names <u>with the endings *–ton, -ham,* or *–wich*</u> come from town names. _____

B. Identifying Misplaced Prepositional Phrases

Underline every prepositional phrase in each sentence once. If a phrase is misplaced, underline it twice.

EXAMPLE Every member wears a cap <u>with a picture</u> <u>of a lizard</u> <u>of the team</u>.

1. Muddy footprints marked the path Sam had taken through the family room and into the kitchen.

2. Squirrels ran up the tree with their mouths full of nuts.

3. Let's stop for pizza after the movie is over.

4. In October, the leaves on the trees begin changing colors.

5. Mrs. Whitaker, beneath the oak tree, planted petunias in neat rows.

6. During the thunderstorm, we ran to the building across the street for shelter.

7. A large committee of students and advisors planned Homecoming in the school library.

8. Under the couch, Dave spotted the cat playing with catnip.

9. The boutique you want is in the west wing at the other end of the mall.

10. The D.J., on his CD player, selected songs for the after-school dance.

Prepositional Phrases

Application

A. Revising Sentences with Misplaced Prepositional Phrases

Rewrite each sentence, changing the position of one or more prepositional phrases so that the sentence is no longer confusing. If there is no error, write **Correct**.

> **EXAMPLE** Without his knowledge, a village clerk sometimes added a descriptive word to the given name of a man.
>
> *A village clerk sometimes added a descriptive word to the given name of a man without his knowledge.*

1. On the hay wagon, the horse pulled the group of students.

_____

2. In the ice, several skaters saw the large crack.

_____

3. A lion startled the hunter with a ferocious roar.

_____

4. The profits were deposited safely in the bank from the bake sale.

_____

5. Through the goal posts fans watched the football sail.

_____

B. Using Prepositional Phrases as Modifiers

The following information tells about famous people in history with distinctive names. Use the information to write complete sentences about these people. Use at least two prepositional phrases in each sentence. Underline each prepositional phrase you use.

1. Who: Eric the Red (so called because of his red hair); **When:** A.D. 985; **What:** This Viking explored and colonized Greenland.

_____

_____

2. Who: Joan of Arc (honored as a heroine in France); **When:** 1429: **What:** This 17-year-old peasant girl led the French army to victory over England at Orleans.

_____

_____

3. Who: Liliuokalani (the name taken by Lydia Kamekeha when she became queen); **Where:** Hawaii, before it was annexed to the U.S.; **When:** 1891 to 1893.

_____

_____

CHAPTER 2

Appositive Phrases

Teaching

An **appositive** is a noun or pronoun that identifies or renames another noun or pronoun. An **appositive phrase** consists of an appositive plus its modifiers.

> Have you heard of the writer <u>Lydia Maria Child</u>? (*Lydia Maria Child* identifies *the writer.*)

> Her best-known work, <u>a poem that begins "Over the river and through the woods</u>," was set to music. (The appositive phrase is underlined.)

An **essential appositive** make the meaning of a sentence clear.

> The abolitionist <u>Child</u> wrote to end slavery. (*Child* identifies which *abolitionist.*)

A **nonessential appositive** adds extra information to a sentence whose meaning is already clear. Use commas to set off nonessential appositive phrases.

> She is also known for starting a magazine for children, <u>the first of its kind</u>.

A. Identifying Appositives and Appositive Phrases

Underline the appositive or appositive phrase in each of the following sentences.

1. The American author Henry David Thoreau lived for a time at Walden Pond.
2. Paula wrote about Edgar Allan Poe, the American poet and short-story writer.
3. John Steinbeck, author of *The Grapes of Wrath,* was raised in California.
4. "God Bless America" was written by the prolific and patriotic composer Irving Berlin.
5. Nathaniel Hawthorne and his friends began their own community, Brook Farm.
6. Will Rogers, a humorist and philosopher, was originally a cowboy.
7. American poet Theodore Roethke received a Pulitzer Prize in 1954.
8. Harriet Beecher Stowe's novel *Uncle Tom's Cabin* describes slavery in the years before the American Civil War.

B. Identifying Essential and Nonessential Appositives

Underline the appositive or appositive phrase in each sentence below. On the line, identify each phrase as **E** if it is essential or **NE** if it is nonessential. Add the necessary commas to sentences with nonessential clauses.

1. The poetry of Robert Frost is identified with rural New England the place where Frost was raised. _____

2. *Spin a Soft Black Song* a book of poetry for young readers was written by Nikki Giovanni. _____

3. Katherine Lee Bates wrote the patriotic hymn "America the Beautiful" after viewing the Rocky Mountains. _____

4. Author and journalist Louis Bromfield lived part of his life on a farm in Ohio. _____

5. The running of the bulls in Pamplona, Spain, was described in Hemingway's book *Death in the Afternoon.* _____

Lesson 2 ## Appositive Phrases   *More Practice*

A. Identifying Appositive Phrases

Underline the appositive phrase in each sentence. Write the noun it identifies to the right. Then identify each phrase as **E** if it is essential or **NE** if it is nonessential, and add commas where they are needed to set off nonessential phrases.

> **EXAMPLE** Maya Angelou, the poet, also teaches. *Maya Angelou, NE*

1. Frederick Douglass established the newspaper *North Star* in 1847. _____

2. *Age of Innocence* a novel by Edith Wharton won a Pulitzer Prize. _____

3. Ohioan James Thurber authored two books of modern fairy tales. _____

4. Zelda Fitzgerald wife of F. Scott Fitzgerald wrote a novel about their marriage. _____

5. The play *A Raisin in the Sun* was the first play produced on Broadway by an African-American woman. _____

6. The play's success brought its writer Lorraine Hansberry instant acclaim. _____

7. Many works of James Fenimore Cooper a prolific author describe the tension between society and the individual. _____

8. *Godey's Lady's Book* an early magazine on manners and fashion was edited by Sarah J. Hale. _____

B. Using Appositives in Sentences

Choose one of the nouns in each sentence that needs clarification or that can be given extra information. Rewrite the sentence, adding an appositive to the noun you chose. Use commas if necessary.

1. My friend wrote a letter to the editor of a newspaper.

_____

2. The secretary circulated the notice to the members of the club.

_____

3. Does the clerk know the price of that book?

_____

4. His brother composed a poem for the literary magazine of his school.

_____

5. Edgar Allan Poe wrote poems, essays, and short stories.

_____

Lesson 2

Appositive Phrases

Application

A. Writing with Appositives and Appositive Phrases

Combine each set of sentences into a single sentence by using appositives or appositive phrases. Use commas as they are needed.

1. As a child, Amy Tan eagerly read books. She especially loved fairy tales and Gothic and Bible stories.

_____

_____

2. Amy's father came to America to escape civil unrest in his homeland. He was an electrical engineer and Baptist minister.

_____

_____

3. Later, Amy better understood her mother. Her mother had been an abused wife who had to abandon her children and flee China before the Communist take-over.

_____

_____

4. *The Joy Luck Club* was translated into 23 languages, including Chinese. It was a world-wide best seller.

_____

_____

B. Using Appositives and Appositive Phrases

You are a member of a club that will award a prize to a famous author. Choose an author whom you particularly like, or invent one. Write a paragraph nominating your author for the award, explaining why he or she should be honored. Use at least three appositives or appositive phrases in your paragraph. After each appositives or appositive phrase, write in parentheses whether it was essential **(E)** or nonessential **(NE)**.

_____

_____

_____

_____

_____

_____

Lesson 3 # Verbals: Participial Phrases

Teaching

A **verbal** is a verb form that acts as a noun, an adjective, or an adverb. A **verbal phrase** consists of a verbal plus its modifiers and complements.

A **participle** is a verbal that acts as an adjective. A **participial phrase** consists of a participle plus its modifiers and complements. Since a participle is formed from a verb, it may have an object. Any object and its modifiers are part of the participial phrase.

> <u>Carrying their backpacks</u>, three students boarded the school bus. (The participle is *Carrying*.)

Participles may be either present participles or past participles. (Present participles always end in *–ing*.

> The passengers <u>standing in the aisle</u> lurched forward. (The present participle is *standing*)

> A <u>broken</u> rail caused the train to leave the track. (The past participle is *broken*)

An **absolute phrase** consists of a participle and the noun or pronoun it modifies. This phrase has no grammatical connection to the sentence in which it appears, although it provides information for the sentence.

> <u>A repair crew having arrived</u>, the supervisor left the scene.

Identifying Participles and Participial Phrases

In each sentence, underline a participle or participial phrase that modifies the boldfaced noun or pronoun. On the blank, write what kind of participle it is: **Pres.** for present participle or **Past** for past participle.

1. The **honeysuckles** blooming in our yard attract swarms of industrious bees. _____

2. Working carefully, the **signpainter** completed the elaborate poster. _____

3. Having about 52,000 people per square mile, **Paris** is among the world's most crowded cities. _____

4. An enormous **icicle,** broken into several pieces, lay on the sidewalk. _____

5. Our new **puppy** finally falling asleep, we crept out of the kitchen. _____

6. In **poetry** written in English, meters are based on syllables and stress. _____

7. The player piano **rolls** stored in my grandparents' attic for 60 years are still usable. _____

8. Impressed by the speaker's sense of urgency, **we** listened intently. _____

9. The **movie** being filmed on that set is already over budget. _____

10. Its **radio** blaring loudly enough to be heard a block away, the old gray car rolled slowly down the street. _____

11. The detectives found **scraps** of material from the thief's jacket caught on a nail. _____

12. Only five of the **students** invited to submit projects did so. _____

CHAPTER 2

Verbals: Participial Phrases   *More Practice*

A. Identifying Participles and Participial Phrases

Underline once the participle or participial phrase in each sentence. Underline twice the word that the participle or participial phrase modifies. On the blank, write what kind of participle it is: **Pres.** for present participle and **Past** for past participle.

1. A roaring sound awakened me from a deep sleep.   _____

2. Bitten on the hand by a dog, Mr. Grimsley sought medical help.   _____

3. Brightly glowing embers illuminated the faces around the campfire.   _____

4. The spider monkey, known for its liveliness, sat listlessly in the corner
   of its cage.   _____

5. Climbing to the top of the hill, Charlene watched the scene below.   _____

6. Caught by the strong gust of wind, she barely could keep her balance.   _____

7. A Navaho blanket woven by hand is truly a work of art.   _____

8. Susan, returning, opened her apartment door and went inside.   _____

9. The hungry dog, found at last, eagerly gobbled the dish of food.   _____

10. Screeching tires announced the arrival of Uncle Fred.   _____

B. Using Participial Phrases to Combine Sentences

Use participial phrases to combine each set of sentences into one sentence. Use an absolute phrase in the even-numbered items.

> **EXAMPLE** The tour boat was already full. We waited for the next trip.
> *The tour boat being full already, we waited for the next trip.*

1. John pulled his carry-on bag from the overhead compartment. He lost his grip
   on it.

   _____

2. Luggage littered the area. We kept on walking through the terminal.

   _____

3. He went biking on a sunny afternoon. He traveled over 20 miles.

   _____

4. The snow blocked the roads. Our travel plans were delayed.

   _____

5. Grandpa's old car was eaten by rust. It crumbled in our hands.

   _____

Verbals: Participial Phrases *Application*

A. Using Participial Phrases to Combine Sentences

Combine each of these pairs of sentences into a single sentence by using participial phrases. In one of the three items, use a participial phrase as part of an absolute phrase. Use a comma after each participial phrase that begins a sentence.

1. A rowboat bobbed gently in the middle of the lake. It soon rocked its two occupants to sleep.

_____

_____

2. A hurricane was building near the coast. All cruise ships stayed in the harbor.

_____

_____

3. The co-pilot took over the controls. He flew the jet while the pilot took a break.

_____

_____

B. Using Participles and Participial Phrases in Writing

On the blank to the right of each item below, write **Pres.** for a present participle and **Past** for a past participle. Then write a sentence using the participle or phrase. Use a comma after each participial phrase that begins a sentence. Use participial phrases within absolute phrases for the even-numbered items.

1. plowing through snow _____

_____

2. being blinded by fog _____

_____

_____

3. crowded with holiday travelers _____

_____

4. missing their connections in Atlanta _____

_____

_____

5. searching for a vegetarian meal _____

_____

CHAPTER 2

Verbals: Gerund Phrases

Teaching

A **gerund** is a verb form that ends in –*ing* and acts as a noun. A **gerund phrase** consists of a gerund plus its modifiers and complements. Since a gerund is formed from a verb, it may have an object. Any object and its modifiers are part of the gerund phrase.

> Basic <u>cooking</u> requires <u>following simple directions</u>.

In sentences, gerunds and gerund phrases may be used anywhere nouns may be used.

> For me, <u>locating the ingredients</u> *(subject)* may take longer than <u>putting them together</u> *(object of preposition)*.

> I dislike <u>beating eggs by hand</u> *(direct object)*.

> My preference is <u>using the electric beaters</u> *(predicate nominative)*.

A. Identifying Gerunds and Gerund Phrases

In each sentence, underline every gerund phrase once. Underline each gerund twice.

1. George's specialty was making a perfect soufflé.
2. Elise began by sifting four cups of wheat flour into a large bowl.
3. Outdoor grilling is popular, especially in the summer.
4. The most difficult task was kneading the dough to the proper consistency.
5. Gary resents having clean-up duty after every holiday or other special occasion.
6. There was no doubt about her winning the prize for best menu.
7. Complimenting the cook is easy when the meal is delicious.
8. Maria's assignment was selecting the perfect menu for the awards banquet.

B. Identifying Gerunds and Gerund Phrases

Underline each gerund or gerund phrase. On the blank to the right of each sentence, write **S** for a subject, **PN** for a predicate nominative, **DO** for a direct object, or **OP** for an object of a preposition.

1. The circus performer's most popular feat was juggling seven bottles at once. _____

2. Commercial fishing must be regulated to prevent depletion of fish populations. _____

3. The doctors were leery of increasing the dosage of the patient's medication. _____

4. The teacher suggested reading the poem at least twice. _____

5. The company prospers by producing software for a variety of businesses. _____

6. An inventor's major concern is ceating an invention that actually works. _____

7. Giving to charity is encouraged by most religions. _____

8. By exercising regularly, people can improve their mental and physical health. _____

9. Writing novels under an assumed name was not unusual in the 19th century. _____

10. Mechanization has dramatically altered traditional farming. _____

Lesson 4

Verbals: Gerund Phrases

More Practice

A. Identifying Gerunds and Gerund Phrases

Underline each gerund or gerund phrase. On the blank to the right of each sentence, write **S** for a subject, **PN** for a predicate nominative, **DO** for a direct object, or **OP** for an object of a preposition.

1. Representing the junior class was her job as a member of the student senate. _____

2. The only problem is finding someone who is prepared to finance the project. _____

3. You can manage large amounts of information by using a computer. _____

4. César enjoys playing guitar with a rock band. _____

5. Searching for underwater wrecks is a dangerous occupation. _____

6. You can access that Web page by clicking here. _____

7. Hauling the large rocks from the riverbank quickly lost its appeal for Jan. _____

8. Kevin considered raising his grades by at least a point. _____

9. Julia was inspired to create her own quilt after viewing the craft exhibit. _____

10. One way to write a believable short story is drawing on your own experience. _____

B. Using Gerunds and Gerund Phrases

Use gerund phrases to combine each set of sentences into one sentence.

1. There was one clear objective in the gourmet cooking class. That was to guide the students to culinary mastery.

_____

2. Jason solved his problem of lack of ingredients. He cut his recipe in half.

_____

3. Mix the batter for five minutes. This produces a light and fluffy dessert.

_____

4. Of all his jobs, Nick had a favorite one. He ground coffee beans at the local coffee house.

_____

5. Freeze blueberries when they are plentiful. This gives you a taste of summer during the winter months.

_____

_____

CHAPTER 2

Verbals: Gerund Phrases

Application

A. Using Gerunds and Gerund Phrases

Write sentences using the following gerunds and gerund phrases as the sentence parts indicated in parentheses.

1. telling the truth (subject) _____

_____

2. painting the garage (object of preposition) _____

_____

3. entering the coal mine (predicate nominative) _____

_____

4. playing chess (direct object) _____

_____

5. acting on stage (your choice of position) _____

_____

B. Using Gerunds and Gerund Phrases in Writing

You are a member of a committee that is raising funds for an animal rights group by producing a vegetarian cookbook. Write a brief introduction for the cookbook, discussing cooking procedures, the purpose of the book, and/or the goals of your group. Use at least six gerunds in your statement. Underline each gerund or gerund phrase you use.

_____

_____

_____

_____

_____

_____

_____

_____

_____

_____

Verbals: Infinitive Phrases

Lesson 5

Teaching

An **infinitive** is a verb form that usually begins with the word *to* and acts as a noun, an adjective, or an adverb. An **infinitive phrase** consists of an infinitive plus its modifiers and complements. Since an infinitive is formed from a verb, it may have an object.

As noun	<u>To keep library records up to date</u> is easy on the computer. (subject of sentence)
	Patrons like <u>to know the location of selected books</u>. (direct object)
As adjective	Current efforts <u>to computerize all library records</u> are making progress. (*To computerize all library records* modifies *efforts*.)
As adverb	The time needed <u>to find a book</u> has been reduced considerably. (*To find a book* modifies *needed*, telling how a thing is needed.)

An infinitive with a modifier between *to* and the verb is called a **split infinitive.** An example is *to quickly find* rather than *to find quickly.* Although split infinitives are acceptable in informal speech and writing, avoid them in formal writing.

A. Identifying Infinitives and Infinitive Phrases

Underline the infinitive phrase once in each sentence. Underline the infinitive twice.

1. To spend a day without encountering some type of computer is impossible.
2. Most retail stores use computers to keep an accurate count of their merchandise in stock.
3. Computer analysis of geological areas helps oil companies to select drilling sites.
4. Giant computerized "arms" help to pour molten steel into molds.
5. Highly specialized computers are needed to navigate spacecrafts.
6. A programming mistake may cause an entire mission to fail.
7. Many animated films use computers to produce high quality pictures.
8. Presently, great strides are being made to design even more complex computers that think for themselves.

B. Identifying Infinitive Phrases

Underline the infinitive phrase in each sentence. On the blank to the right of each sentence, **N** for a noun, **ADJ** for an adjective, or **ADV** for an adverb.

1. The selection committee plans to evaluate the qualifications of the candidates. _____

2. To combat rabies is one reason for inoculating pets. _____

3. The owner of the amusement park uses admission fees to pay his property taxes. _____

4. The purpose of the gathering was to celebrate the town's bicentennial. _____

5. The Great Wall of China was built to protect China from northern invaders. _____

6. The president of the company asked her to call a meeting. _____

7. Maoris, the first people to inhabit New Zealand, belong to the Polynesian race. _____

8. Unfortunately, we arrived too late to catch the beginning of the show. _____

Verbals: Infinitive Phrases

More Practice

A. Identifying Infinitive Phrases

Underline the infinitive phrase in each sentence. On the blank to the right of each sentence, write **N** for a noun, **ADJ** for an adjective, or **ADV** for an adverb.

1. This word processing program is not difficult to use. _____

2. What is to be gained from the use of word processing? _____

3. To make additions, deletions, and corrections is quite easy. _____

4. You will easily learn to rearrange pieces of text. _____

5. As a result, you are free to make changes almost endlessly. _____

6. When the time to produce a final copy arrives, the printer performs the task automatically. _____

7. There is no longer any need to retype pages of text. _____

8. A word-processing system enables you to store your text for future use. _____

9. To produce multiple copies of form letters is a simple task. _____

10. The original purpose of word-processing systems was simply to produce written material faster and easier. _____

11. Now, even elementary schools students use computers to do their homework. _____

12. In fact, more advanced word-processing skills include the ability to add charts and line art to a document. _____

B. Using Infinitive Phrases

Write a sentence using each of the following infinitive phrases.

1. to explore a deep cave

_____

2. to arrive on time

_____

3. to remember the words of old songs

_____

4. to listen to country music

_____

5. to watch a parade

_____

Lesson 5

Verbals: Infinitive Phrases   *Application*

A. Using Infinitive Phrases to Combine Sentences

Combine each pair of sentences below, changing one of the sentences into an infinitive phrase. Add, drop, or change words as needed.

> **EXAMPLE** In this novel, a thief plans his next crime. He will rob a bank.
> *In this novel, a thief plans to rob a bank.*

1. We can aid famine victims. One way is by publicizing their plight internationally.

_____

2. After much thought she set a goal. She would become a biomedical engineer.

_____

3. You can make a difference. Here is how: register, vote, and volunteer for the political party of your choice.

_____

4. The class decided it would raise money for the flood victims. The entire class agreed with the decision.

_____

5. An overpowering urge gripped me. I wanted to sing loudly.

_____

B. Using Infinitive Phrases for Variety

How do you use computers? Where do you use them? Is it easy or difficult for you to use computers? Write a paragraph about you and computers. Use infinitive phrases in at least four of the sentences.

_____

_____

_____

_____

_____

_____

_____

_____

_____

CHAPTER 2

Avoiding Problems with Phrases

Teaching

A **misplaced modifier** is a word or phrase that is placed so far from the word it modifies that the meaning of the sentence is unclear or incorrect.

> **EXAMPLE** Chewing her slipper, Annie found her new puppy. (Was Annie chewing the slipper?)
>
> **REVISION** Annie found her new puppy chewing her slipper.

A **dangling modifier** is a word or phrase that does not clearly modify any noun or pronoun in a sentence.

> **EXAMPLE** Finding her puppy, he was chewing Annie's slipper. (Who was finding the puppy?)
>
> **REVISION** Finding her puppy, Annie caught him chewing her slipper.

A. Finding the Words Modified by Misplaced Phrases

Each underlined phrase is misplaced. On the line to the right, write the word that the phrase is meant to modify.

1. Meatloaf was served to the guests <u>decorated with parsley</u>. _____

2. Allen was writing a report on elephants <u>in the lunchroom</u>. _____

3. The package belonged to the man <u>with the red bow</u>. _____

4. They passed an entire family of raccoons <u>riding their bikes down the path</u>. _____

5. <u>Spurting thick puffs of black smoke</u>, the pilot brought down the damaged plane. _____

6. Ivan noticed the stray dog <u>looking out his window</u>. _____

B. Identifying Misplaced and Dangling Phrases

In each of these sentences, decide whether there is a misplaced or dangling phrase. If there is a problem with a phrase, underline the phrase and write **Misplaced** or **Dangling**. If the sentence is correct, write **Correct** on the line to the right.

1. To play the guitar well, frequent practice is needed. _____

2. Marjorie watched the snow starting to fall through her window. _____

3. In glowing shades of crimson and violet, we admired the sun set. _____

4. Running to catch the bus, the traffic light changed. _____

5. To memorize his part in the play, Brad repeated the lines several times. _____

6. Reading for one more hour, the book was finally finished. _____

7. I discovered a pearly nautilus and several sand dollars walking along the deserted beach. _____

Avoiding Problems with Phrases *More Practice*

Correcting Misplaced and Dangling Phrases

If a sentence contains a misplaced or dangling phrase, rewrite it to eliminate the error. If the sentence is correct, write **Correct.**

1. A trainer helped Joyce to run faster.

_____

2. Sagging on one side, Art looked warily at the barn door.

_____

3. Near the peeled onions, tears flowed.

_____

4. To dance well the muscles must be toned.

_____

5. Mrs. Humphrey, breathing heavily, climbed the steep stairs.

_____

6. To learn chess, books are very helpful.

_____

7. The parade, holding colorful banners, was filled with hundreds of marchers.

_____

8. Is the large red umbrella in the utility room or in the closet?

_____

9. Exhausted, the bed looked very inviting.

_____

10. Darrell kept his composure throughout the harrowing ordeal.

_____

11. To wash the car, a special soap did the job.

_____

12. In the tree, we watched the woodpecker drilling.

_____

CHAPTER 2

Lesson 6

Avoiding Problems with Phrases

Application

A. Correcting Misplaced and Dangling Phrases

If a sentence contains a misplaced or dangling phrase, rewrite it to eliminate the error. If the sentence is correct, write **Correct**. Remember that an absolute phrase may be correct.

1. Lasting more than four years, over eight million soldiers' lives were claimed by World War I.

_____

2. Countries before the assassination of the Archduke of Austria-Hungary of Europe had chosen sides.

_____

3. Russian troops having mobilized along the German border, Germany declared war against Russia in August of 1914.

_____

_____

4. The fighting ended when Germany accepted the armistice terms the Allied Forces had been demanding on November 11, 1918.

_____

_____

B. Correcting Misplaced and Dangling Phrases in Writing

In this paragraph, find the misplaced or dangling phrases. On the lines below, write the numbers of the sentences with phrase problems, and rewrite those sentences correctly.

   (1) Easter Island, one of many islands in the South Pacific, has a special distinction. **(2)** Approaching the area by sea or air, huge statues are visible. **(3)** Cut from volcanic rock, you are astounded by the size of these sculptures. **(4)** Ranging in height from 14 to 65 feet, you are amazed by spectacular carvings. **(5)** Most historians believe the statues to have been made by prehistoric Polynesians. **(6)** These remarkable artisans quarried and carved the several ton figures using primitive tools.

_____

_____

_____

_____

_____

CHAPTER 2

Lesson 7 · Sentence Diagramming: Phrases

A. Prepositional Phrases

A career as a set designer can appeal to a person with imagination and artistic ability.

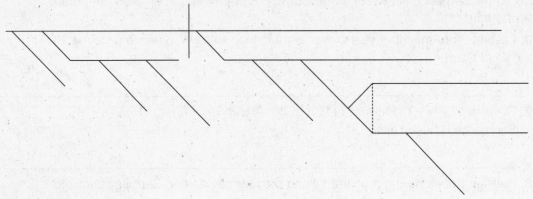

B. Appositive Phrases

The set design, a major element in a play's success, sets the mood of a play.

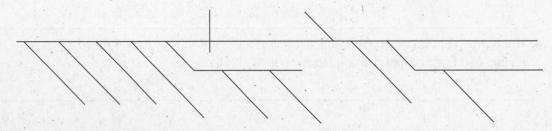

C. Participial Phrases

The designer, keeping in mind the requirements of the play, plans each element on the stage.

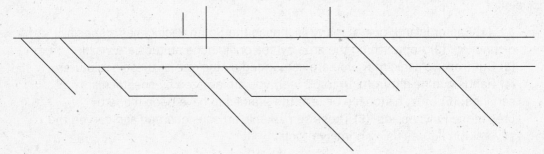

Sentence Diagramming

Lesson 7

D. Gerund Phrases

Finding the right furniture of a particular time period can be a challenge for the set crew.

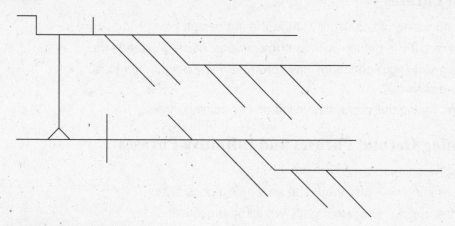

E. Infinitive Phrases

Infinitive Phrase as Subject To get the right effect requires effort.

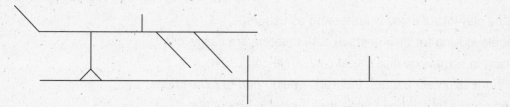

Infinitive Phrase as Direct Object Would you like to go into stage design?

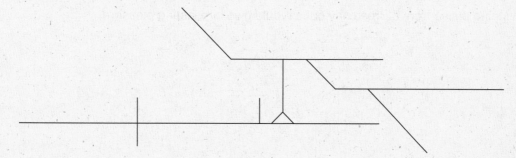

CHAPTER 2

Lesson 7

Sentence Diagramming

Application

On a separate piece of paper, diagram each of the following sentences.

A. Diagramming Prepositional, Appositive, and Participial Phrases

1. Reviewing a new play, critics usually judge the set design.
2. The local drama critic, a person with strong opinions, has high standards.
3. Her columns reviewing productions have brought many people, her loyal readers, to the plays.
4. My friend Jim, hating dull plays, has relied on her opinion often.

B. Diagramming Gerund Phrases and Infinitive Phrases

1. Can you imagine going to plays for your job?
2. Finding a fascinating new play would be an enticing possibility.
3. To expect a fascinating new play nightly would be unrealistic.
4. Most of us prefer to wait for the reviews.

C. Mixed Practice

1. Many play-lovers enjoy volunteering as ushers.
2. People looking for their seats in dark theaters are easily lost.
3. Sitting in somebody else's seat can cause confusion.
4. Without volunteer ushers, theaters would need to raise prices.
5. Many playwrights hope to see their works in production.
6. A writer known locally for his comedies, Luke Colombi, is a graduate from my high school.
7. To gain a wider reputation is Luke's goal.
8. Winning praise from a Broadway critic would give him lasting pleasure.

Kinds of Clauses

Teaching

A **clause** is a group of words that contains both a subject and a verb. An **independent clause,** also known as a **main clause,** expresses a complete thought and can stand alone as a sentence.

> Grocery <u>stores</u> <u>require</u> accurate records of their inventory.
>   SUBJECT   VERB

A **subordinate clause,** also called a **dependent clause,** contains a subject and a verb but does not express a complete thought and cannot stand alone as a sentence.

> before a <u>product</u> <u>runs</u> out (What happens at this time?)
>   SUBJECT VERB

A subordinate clause must always be combined with an independent clause.

> <u>A store must reorder stock</u> <u>before a product runs out</u>.
> INDEPENDENT CLAUSE   SUBORDINATE CLAUSE

Two kinds of words that link or introduce clauses are subordinating conjunctions and coordinating conjunctions. A **coordinating conjunction** joins two independent clauses. Examples of coordinating conjunctions are *and, or, but*, and *yet*.

> Stores always needed accurate records, **but** they didn't have the technology.

A **subordinating conjunction** introduces a subordinate clause.

> **After** lasers and computers were invented, these machines solved the problem.

The following are examples of subordinating conjunctions: *after, although, as, because, before, if, in order that, provided, since, so that, until, when, where, wherever, while*.

Identifying Kinds of Clauses and Conjunctions

On the line after each sentence, identify the boldfaced group of words by writing **IND** for an independent clause or **SUB** for a subordinate clause. Then find the conjunction in the sentence. Underline a coordinating conjunction once and underline a subordinating conjunction twice.

1. Customers demand thousands of products, and **every grocery tries to please.** _____

2. Because people have different tastes, **stores order many brands.** _____

3. **When a product is popular,** a store stocks many sizes of that one product. _____

4. In the past, a cashier could not record every product sold **as she rang up a sale.** _____

5. While the store was closed, **workers took inventory.** _____

6. **Managers noted products low in stock,** and the purchasing agent reordered. _____

7. **If stock ran out too soon,** customers complained. _____

8. In 1948, **when a graduate student at Drexel Institute of Technology heard about the problem,** he and a partner set out to solve it. _____

9. Almost 25 years passed **before their solution became practical.** _____

Kinds of Clauses

More Practice

A. Identifying Conjunctions and Kinds of Clauses

In these sentences, underline every independent clause once, underline every conjunction twice, and place parentheses around every subordinate clause. Not every sentence has more than one clause.

1. Although sea anemones resemble plants, they are actually animals.
2. I was eager to visit Greece because I had heard so much about its scenery.
3. He was not impressed by scenic views, but he had never seen the Grand Canyon.
4. Before they began their trek across Antarctica, the explorers checked their supplies.
5. Because of thick forests inland, the country's cities are located on the coast.
6. Many people love camping, yet others won't go near a tent.
7. Because it is nocturnal, the badger is rarely seen by day.
8. Lin could hike alone in the woods, or she could walk her dog in the park.
9. Since I planted the trumpet vine, we have had hummingbirds in the garden.
10. The Wrights are picking apples today, and they will start making cider tomorrow.

B. Identifying Independent and Subordinate Clauses

Each sentence below contains two clauses and a conjunction. Underline the conjunction and write above it either **CC** for coordinating conjunction or **SC** for subordinating conjunction. Above each clause write **IND** for independent or **SUB** for subordinate.

1. When inventors developed the first bar code, they used elements from movie soundtracks and Morse code.

2. Soundtracks were printed on the edge of the movie film, and light passing through the film was converted to sound.

3. If light could "read" a soundtrack, it could read a bar code too.

4. Light passes through a film, but it has to bounce off a bar code label.

5. After the light bounced off the inventors' label, it entered an oscilloscope.

6. Although the inventors' idea worked in experiments, it required a very bright light.

7. The idea would not work until the laser was invented.

8. Scientists tested many forms of bar codes before they chose the current system.

Lesson 1

Kinds of Clauses

Application

A. Using Clauses in Writing

Use each group of words below in two different sentences. First use it as an independent clause, adding another independent clause either before or after it, and using an appropriate coordinating conjunction. Second, add a subordinating conjunction to the word group and use it as a subordinate clause, joining it to a new independent clause.

1. most groceries stock several cereal brands

_____

_____

2. this bread is inexpensive

_____

_____

3. I prefer seedless oranges

_____

_____

4. she usually buys frozen peas

_____

_____

5. this aisle offers hundreds of canned foods

_____

_____

B. Building Sentences with Clauses

Beginning with the following sentence, add clauses as described in parentheses.
At each step, add the new element to the preceding answer to make one sentence.

Every store keeps many products in stock.

1. (Add a conjunction and an independent clause.) _____

_____

2. (Add a conjunction and a subordinate clause.) _____

_____

3. (Add a conjunction and another clause, either independent or subordinate.) _____

_____

CHAPTER 3

Adjective Clauses and Adverb Clauses

Teaching

Lesson 2

An **adjective clause** is a subordinate clause that modifies a noun or pronoun. Like an adjective, it tells *which one* or *what kind.* An adjective clause may be called a **relative clause,** and the word that introduces it is either a **relative pronoun** or a **relative adverb.** Examples of relative pronouns are *who, whom, whose, that,* and *which.* Relative adverbs include *after, before, when,* and *where.*

> The Pulitzer Prize is the award <u>that is most desired by journalists</u>. (*Which* award?)

An **essential adjective clause,** as in the example above, provides information that is necessary to identify the noun or pronoun it modifies. A **nonessential clause** provides additional, but not needed, information. Use commas to set off a nonessential clause.

> Who won this year's Pulitzer Prizes, <u>which were awarded in April</u>? (nonessential)

An **adverb clause** is a subordinate clause that modifies a verb, adjective, or adverb. Like an adverb, it tells *where, when, why, how,* or *to what extent.* Adverb clauses are usually introduced by **subordinating conjunctions** such as *before, when, because, since, as, than, if, though, until, so that, as, as if, where, wherever.*

> <u>If you win</u>, your reputation rises. (*Why* does your reputation rise? Modifies verb)

Sometimes words in an adverb clause that repeat or almost repeat words in the main clause are not stated, but only implied. Such clauses are called **elliptical.**

> Winning writers are regarded more highly <u>than others</u>. (than others are regarded)

Identifying Adjective and Adverb Clauses

For sentences 1 through 8, underline the adjective clause or adverb clause that modifies the boldfaced word(s). For the remaining sentences, underline the adjective clause or adverb clause once and underline the word(s) modified twice.

1. The **Pulitzer Prizes,** which were founded by newspaper publisher Joseph Pulitzer, recognize excellent writing in journalism and other fields.

2. William Faulkner **won** two Pulitzer Prizes after he won the Nobel Prize.

3. **Joseph Pulitzer,** who spent his life as a journalist, left funds at his death for prizes in journalism.

4. The **year** 1904, when two writers won the Nobel Prize in Literature, was unusual.

5. The Pulitzer Prize is the **award** that all biographers consider the greatest honor.

6. He never **felt** successful as a poet until he won the Pulitzer Prize.

7. Alfred Nobel **established** his literary prize so that great achievements would be rewarded.

8. If he had not invented dynamite, Nobel **might have never created** his peace prize.

9. Toni Morrison, whose novel *Beloved* won the Pulitzer Prize, was awarded the Nobel Prize in literature.

10. Because Alfred Nobel died on December 10, 1896, the Nobel Prize in literature is awarded on December 10.

11. Alice McDermott, who won the National Book Award, has written four novels.

Adjective Clauses and Adverb Clauses

Lesson 2

More Practice

A. Identifying Adjective Clauses, Adverb Clauses, and Introductory Words

In each sentence, underline the adjective clause or adverb clause once. Underline the word modified twice. On the line, write the relative pronoun or relative adverb that introduces the adjective clause, or the subordinating conjunction that introduces the adverb clause.

> **EXAMPLE** That was the <u>time</u> <u>when she was writing her first novel.</u> *when*

1. Upton Sinclair, who wrote *The Jungle,* was an active social and
   political reformer. _____

2. Show me the places where you planted the tulip bulbs. _____

3. As she walked onto the stage, the actress forgot her opening lines. _____

4. Tasmania, which is an island, belongs to the Australian commonwealth. _____

5. Since wood was scarce on the Great Plains, pioneer families built
   sod houses. _____

6. We waited for Dad where he had dropped us off. _____

7. The book that Raoul is writing may be published next year. _____

8. I always need more time for research than Jennifer. _____

B. Identifying Adverb Clauses and Elliptical Clauses

Below, write the numbers of the sentences in Exercise A that belong in each group.

1. Adverb clauses _____

2. Adverb clauses that are also elliptical clauses _____

C. Identifying Nonessential Clauses

Underline the adjective clause in each of the following sentences. If the clause is nonessential, insert commas where they are needed.

1. The Newbery Medal is awarded to American authors who write outstanding
   children's books.

2. The Newbery Medal which was established in 1921 was named for John
   Newbery.

3. John Newbery who was an English publisher printed the first books for children.

4. Newbery whose patronage aided many writers was called the "friend of
   children."

5. *The Summer of the Swans* is one book that has won the Newbery Medal.

6. Frederic Melcher who established the Newbery Medal also founded the
   Caldecott Medal for illustrators of children's books.

CHAPTER 3

Lesson 2

Adjective Clauses and Adverb Clauses *Application*

A. Using Adjective Clauses to Combine Sentences

Combine each numbered pair of sentences to form one sentence containing an adjective clause that modifies the boldfaced word. If the clause is nonessential, add commas. If the clause is essential, do not add commas.

1. Nobel Prizes are awarded to **individuals.** The winners have made valuable contributions to the "good of mankind."

   _____

2. The first **Caldecott Medal** was awarded to Dorothy Lathrop. The medal was designed by Rene Chambellan.

   _____

3. A Pulitzer Prize is also awarded to the best American **play.** The play deals with American life.

   _____

4. **Pearl S. Buck** is an American novelist. She won the Nobel Prize in 1938.

   _____

5. John Berryman wrote ***Seventy-Seven Dream Songs.*** It won the Pulitzer Prize for poetry in 1965.

   _____

B. Using Adverb Clauses to Develop Sentences

Rewrite each of the following sentences, adding an adverb clause that begins with the word in parentheses. If the clause comes at the beginning or the middle of the sentence, set it off with commas. If it comes at the end of the sentence, do not use commas.

1. The Caldecott Medal is awarded for children's picture books. (Use *so that.*)

   _____

2. It helps to outline the setting, plot, and main characters. (Use *before.*)

   _____

3. The Nobel Prize is not awarded for a particular year. (Use *if.*)

   _____

4. I tend to look up prize-winning books at the library. (Use *whenever.*)

   _____

5. Joseph Pulitzer established his literary prizes. (Use *because.*)

   _____

6. Many people like to browse in bookstores. (Use *where.*)

   _____

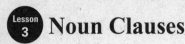

Noun Clauses

Teaching

A **noun clause** is a subordinate clause that is used as a noun. Noun clauses may be used in the same ways nouns are used, including as the object of a verbal or as an appositive.

Subject	<u>What early microscopes revealed</u> astonished people.
Direct object	They learned <u>that tiny animals swam in drinking water</u>.
Indirect object	Doubters gave <u>whoever reported the news</u> a hard time.
Predicate nominative	To them, the tiny animals were <u>what someone made up</u>.
Object of a preposition	We are still amazed by <u>how little we know about animals</u>.
Direct object of gerund	Biologists report finding <u>what was never seen before</u>.
Appositive	Finding new creatures, <u>which can happen</u>, excites us.

Usually, a noun clause is introduced by one of these words: a **relative pronoun,** such as *what, whatever, who, whom, whoever, whomever,* and *which;* or a **subordinating conjunction,** such as *how, that, when, where, whether,* and *why.*

Identifying Noun Clauses and Their Uses

Underline the noun clause in each sentence. Then circle the initials in parentheses that identify how the noun clause is used: **S** for subject, **DO** for direct object, **IO** for indirect object, **PN** for predicate nominative, **OP** for object of a preposition, **DOV** for direct object of a verbal, or **APP** for an appositive.

1. That a secretive lynx lives in this area has long been suspected. **(S, PN, APP)**

2. The counselors offered whoever saw a mountain lion a ride home. **(S, DO, IO)**

3. The researchers knew that emperor penguins were seldom seen in their natural habitat. **(DO, PN, OP)**

4. Whoever sees a dead leaf mantis must have a good eye for camouflage. **(APP, DOV, S)**

5. You would be surprised by how many one-celled animals you can see in a drop of pond water under a microscope. **(OP, DO, PN)**

6. Finding where musk ox graze means a trip to the remote tundra. **(OP, PN, DOV)**

7. Risa showed whoever was interested her slides of the slow loris. **(IO, DO, APP)**

8. Amoebas and paramecia were what confused the student. **(PN, DO, IO)**

9. He heard that the solitary loon lived on this remote lake. **(S, PN, DO)**

10. The spelunkers were shocked at how many bats hung hidden deep in the cave. **(PN, DO, OP)**

11. To see how the African lung fish builds its mud cocoon was fascinating. **(OP, DOV, S)**

12. Small many-celled animals, whatever you call them, are among nature's strangest creatures. **(S, APP, IO)**

Name _____ Date _____

Noun Clauses

Lesson 3

More Practice

A. Identifying Noun Clauses and Their Uses

Underline the noun clause in each sentence. Then, on the line identify it and write
S for subject, **DO** for direct object, **IO** for indirect object, **PN** for predicate
nominative, **OP** for object of a preposition, **DOV** for direct object of a verbal
(gerund, participle, or infinitive) and **APP** for appositive.

1. The candidate gave whomever he met a firm handshake and a winning smile.   _____

2. Whether an actual person named Homer wrote *The Odyssey* is still unknown.   _____

3. Everyone wants to know how the magician made her assistant disappear.   _____

4. Some scientists believe that dinosaurs may have been warm-blooded.   _____

5. I have no information about whose boots these are.   _____

6. My only question is why he needs our sleeping bags.   _____

7. Her poems focus on our best qualities, whatever is praiseworthy in humans.   _____

B. Using Noun Clauses

Use each of these clauses as a noun clause in an original sentence. In parentheses
after your sentence, write how the noun clause is used.

a. whoever shot the endangered rhinoceros

d. that little brown bats slept there

b. how seldom we see the ovenbird

e. why he spent years studying coelacanths

c. what animals live in a coral reef

f. where the panda hides

1. _____

_____

2. _____

_____

3. _____

_____

4. _____

_____

5. _____

_____

6. _____

_____

Noun Clauses

Application

A. Using Noun Clauses

Revise this paragraph, replacing each noun clause with a new noun clause that adds new details or changes the story in some way. In parentheses after each revised clause, write how the noun clause is used.

The students had not realized that so many species were still undiscovered. Finding new species, which could happen on this trip, was what everyone hoped for. Whoever discovered a new beetle or ant (maybe even a reptile) would be the hero of the trip. However, new discoveries were not guaranteed. Their leader, Professor Robinson, told whoever thought it would be easy a much different story.

_____

_____

_____

_____

_____

B. Using Noun Clauses in Writing

You are a scientist writing a proposal for funds to investigate whether the Loch Ness monster is a surviving dinosaur. Write at least two paragraphs of your proposal, using at least four noun clauses. Underline each noun clause.

_____

_____

_____

_____

_____

_____

_____

_____

_____

_____

_____

Lesson 4 Sentence Structure

Teaching

A **simple sentence** has one independent clause and no subordinate clauses. Any part of the sentence, such as subject, predicate, verb, or object, may be compound.

<u>Shape</u> and <u>composition</u> are used to classify volcanes. (compound subject)

A **compound sentence** has two or more independent clauses joined together. Any of these can be used to join independent clauses: a coordinating conjunction, a semicolon, or a semicolon followed by a conjunctive adverb.

<u>Some volcanoes are active; however, others are dormant, or sleeping</u>.

A **complex sentence** has one independent clause and one or more subordinate clauses.

<u>When a volcano erupts underwater many times, it may pile up rock that eventually reaches the water's surface and forms an island.</u>

A **compound-complex sentence** consists of two or more independent clauses and one or more subordinate clauses.

<u>Mainland United States has very few active volcanoes; therefore, when even a limited eruption occurs, the event becomes front-page news.</u>

Identifying Kinds of Sentences

Identify each sentence below by writing **S** for simple, **CD** for compound, **CX** for complex, or **CC** for compound-complex.

1. The word volcano comes from Vulcan, the name of the Roman god of fire. _____

2. Most volcanoes are located in areas of weakness in the earth's crust where internal pressure occasionally breaks through. _____

3. Many volcanoes form mountains, but others are just cracks in the ground. _____

4. Over the last few centuries, volcanoes have caused thousands of deaths. _____

5. The eruption of Krakatau produced tidal waves that rose over 100 feet high; the waves drowned about 36,000 people! _____

6. The lava that is spewed forth by volcanoes consists of molten rock. _____

7. In Iceland, planes take tourists to view volcanic eruptions. _____

8. Prehistoric volcanoes were far more violent than those in recorded history have been; in fact, a giant volcano is blamed for the extinction of the dinosaurs. _____

9. When Mount St. Helens in Washington erupted, it killed 65 people. _____

10. Volcanoes are not unique to Earth; many other heavenly bodies show evidence of even more violent volcanoes. _____

11. There is little doubt that volcanoes are among the most destructive natural forces, yet they also provide benefits to mankind. _____

12. Volcanic materials are used in industry, and volcanic steam can generate power. _____

Lesson 4 — Sentence Structure

More Practice

A. Identifying Kinds of Sentences

Identify each sentence below by writing **S** for simple, **CD** for compound, **CX** for complex, or **CC** for compound-complex.

1. Flying like a bat, a chimney swift is almost always in the air. _____

2. Because a swift's tail is so short, it cannot be seen unless it is spread. _____

3. When swifts rest, their short, spiny tails help them prop themselves against the inside walls of chimneys. _____

4. As they glide between spurts of wing flapping, they hold their wings bowed, and they sometimes make chirping sounds. _____

5. Swifts feed on insects in the air. _____

6. A chimney swift may fly 135,000 miles a year, and for short distances its speed may be over 100 miles per hour. _____

B. Using Different Kinds of Sentences

Combine each set of sentences into one sentence of the type indicated in parentheses.

1. (compound) Wind at 8 to 12 miles per hour is a gentle breeze. Wind above 75 miles per hour is a hurricane.

_____

2. (complex) Warm air moves upward. Cooler air moves in to replace it.

_____

3. (compound-complex) Hurricanes hit the coast. Most people move inland. Some people always stay behind.

_____

_____

4. (simple) Tornadoes can be very destructive. Hurricanes can cause massive destruction.

_____

5. (complex) Summer monsoons travel from the cooler sea to the warmer land. Summer monsoons are called wet monsoons.

_____

6. (compound) A dry monsoon travels from land to sea. A wet monsoon travels from sea to land.

_____

CHAPTER 3

Sentence Structure

Application

A. Using Different Structures to Combine Sentences

Combine the ideas expressed in the simple sentences of this paragraph into no more than five sentences. In parentheses after each sentence, label what kind of sentence you used: **CP** for compound, **CX** for complex, or **CC** for compound-complex.

> A novel is a work of fiction. It can contain both real and imaginary characters. The people in the story are the characters. Characters provide a central focus for the events. They perform the action. Things happen to them. Plot tells what happens to the characters. A plot usually has a beginning, middle, and end. The theme is the basic idea of the novel. Style is the author's way of writing.

_____

_____

_____

_____

_____

_____

_____

_____

B. Using Different Sentence Structures in Directions

Write a paragraph of directions for writing a novel. Include at least one of each kind of sentence: simple, compound, complex, and compound-complex. Label in parentheses the sentence type: **S, CD, CX,** or **CC.**

_____

_____

_____

_____

_____

_____

_____

_____

_____

CHAPTER 3

Lesson 5 — Fragments and Run-Ons

Teaching

A **sentence** must have both a subject and a verb, and express a complete thought. A **sentence fragment** is only part of a sentence.

A **phrase fragment** is missing both a subject, a verb, or both.

> **Fragment**   On the highway, fortunately not at rush hour.
>
> **Revision**   The light plane landed on the highway, fortunately not at rush hour.

A **clause fragment** consists of a subordinate clause, which has a subject and verb but does not express a complete thought.

> **Fragment**   Five minutes after the plane landed.
>
> **Revision**   Five minutes after the plane landed, reporters were on the scene.

Other kinds of fragments lack either a subject or a verb.

> **Fragment**   The plane just behind two trucks.
>
> **Revision**   The plane stopped just behind two trucks.

A **run-on sentence** is made up of two or more sentences written as if they were one sentence. Often run-ons have a **comma splice,** the incorrect joining of two sentences by a comma. Correct a run-on by separating the sentences or by joining them correctly with a comma and coordinating conjunction, a semicolon, or a semicolon and conjunctive adverb

> **Run-on**   The pilot was skillful, the plane didn't hit any vehicles on the road.
>
> **Revision**   The pilot was skillful; the plane didn't hit any vehicles on the road.

Identifying Sentences, Sentence Fragments, and Run-ons

On the line to the right of each word group below, write **S, F,** or **R** to identify the word group as a complete sentence, a fragment, or a run-on sentence.

1. Which can land on water or on the ground. _____

2. A single-engine plane has one engine a twin-engine has two. _____

3. The pilot who flies the plan. _____

4. The flight deck has hundreds of instruments. _____

5. A jet is speeding overhead it's too high for me to see but I can hear it, can't you? _____

6. Eight thousand feet above sea level. _____

7. The Curtiss N-4 was an early bi-plane, the De Havilland Comet was an early jet, you can see them both in the aviation museum. _____

8. During World War II, when America built over 300,000 airplanes. _____

9. In 1947, Chuck Yeager flew the first supersonic rocket-powered airplane. _____

10. Flying at an altitude of 10,000 feet and a speed of Mach 2. _____

CHAPTER 3

Fragments and Run-Ons

More Practice

A. Identifying and Correcting Fragments and Run-Ons

On the line after each word group below, write **S, F,** or **R** to identify the word group as a complete sentence, a fragment, or a run-on sentence. Then rewrite each fragment or run-on as one or more correct sentences. Add sentence parts as needed.

1. After an entire day of studying math. _____

_____

2. A picture fell off the wall. _____

_____

3. My aunt invited us to a picnic it's sure to rain that Saturday. _____

_____

4. These books are overdue at the library, I took them out for research for my paper. _____

_____

5. Once was located on Chester Street. _____

_____

B. Correcting Fragments and Run-ons

Rewrite this paragraph, correcting each underlined fragment and run-on. You may add words to any fragment to make it a sentence, or combine it with another sentence. To correct a run-on, you may either separate the sentences or join them correctly.

The Wright brothers owned a bicycle repair shop in Ohio, they built gliders, they tested them in Kitty Hawk, North Carolina. In 1902 they built a successful glider. During that summer, in more than a thousand flights. They glided 600 feet. Several times. In 1903, they flew a gasoline powered plane, it traveled 120 feet in the air, it stayed in the air 12 seconds.

_____

_____

_____

_____

_____

_____

_____

_____

Fragments and Run-Ons

Application

A. Proofreading for Fragments and Run-ons

Rewrite this paragraph, correcting each fragment and run-on.

Astronomy, the study of the sun, moon, planets, and stars. It has many facets. You can study the distances between heavenly bodies, you can study the structure of stars, you can study the nature of the universe. Using many different tools. A telescope, which allows you to see objects from a great distance. A spectrograph separates starlight into various objects, a radio telescope measures radio waves from space.

_____

_____

_____

_____

_____

_____

B. Recognizing and Revising Fragments and Run-ons

The following paragraph has so many fragments that it is impossible to translate with any certainty. Choose and circle one of the possible speakers. Then rewrite the paragraph as if you were that speaker addressing the others. Make up whatever information you need to make the paragraph understandable. Correct all run-ons as well as fragments.

travel agent   traveler   tour leader   resident of the area visited

Watching the sunset. While the tour bus burned in the parking lot. It was a beautiful sight. I thought. Taking pictures of the scene. Everyone in a state of shock. Wondering what would happen next. Picture yourself at a roaring bonfire on the beach. A once-in-a-lifetime experience. Running for help and flapping their arms on the beach. Only the penguins. Sunning on the distant rocks seemed calm.

_____

_____

_____

_____

_____

_____

CHAPTER 3

Lesson 6 **Sentence Diagramming**   *More Practice 1*

Complete each diagram with the sentence provided.

A. Compound Sentences

Clocks and calendars give all of us problems, but living without them is almost unimaginable.

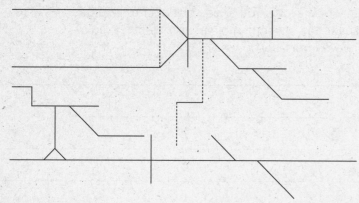

B. Complex Sentences

Adjective Clause Introduced by a Relative Pronoun Certainly, people who relied on a sundial could not expect to get to meetings at a specific minute.

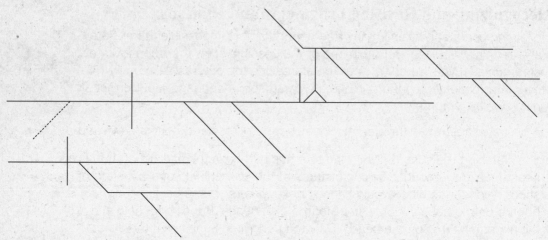

Adjective Clause Introduced by a Relative Adverb With no cars, trains, or planes, meeting attendees could give truthful reasons why they were late by a day or two.

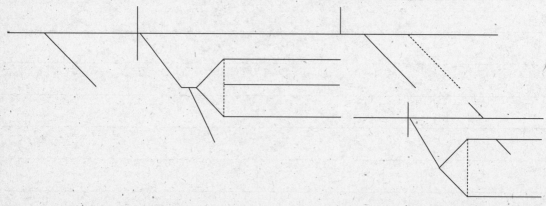

Lesson
6

Sentence Diagramming

More Practice 2

B. Complex Sentences *(continued)*

Adverb Clause If a day is cloudy, sundials are of little use.

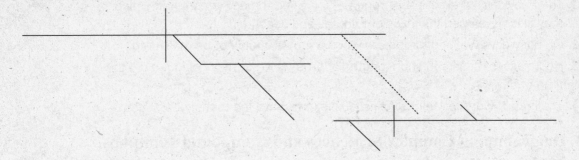

Noun Clauses Whoever sailed over the ocean needed accurate information about how late the time was.

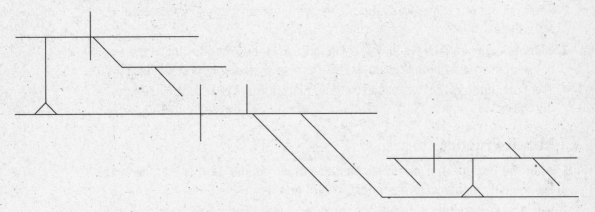

C. Compound-Complex Sentences

A ship's navigator determined where the ship was by comparing the time and position of stars, so he needed the accurate time.

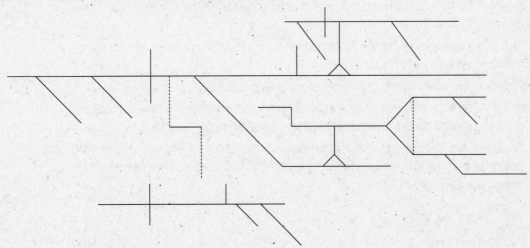

Lesson 6 Sentence Diagramming

Application

On a separate piece of paper, diagram each of the following sentences.

A. Diagramming Compound Sentences and Complex Sentences

1. The Babylonians, excellent astronomers, divided the day into 24 hours, and they also developed the ideas of minutes and seconds.

2. On busy days we long for the era when minutes could not be measured.

3. Hourglasses measured short lengths of time well, but they could not tell the time of day.

4. The French word for bell, which is *cloche,* may have led to the word *clock.*

B. Diagramming Complex Sentences and Compound-Complex Sentences

1. How the Babylonians divided the day into hours, minutes, and seconds is remarkable.

2. The idea of time zones was introduced when trains needed coordinated schedules.

3. Before people could travel quickly over long distances, nobody was upset by differences in local timekeeping, so every town marked noon at a different time.

4. The face of the clock was based on how astronomers divided a circle into 360 parts.

C. Mixed Practice

1. After the Babylonians, centuries passed before people developed mechanical clocks that could accurately measure seconds.

2. What gave clocks their name was the bells that early timepieces struck at each hour.

3. By the 1700s we had clocks that told time accurately to the minute, but today's clocks are more precise.

4. A water clock was a device that measured time by dripping water from one container to another.

5. The original reason why the Royal Greenwich Observatory in England was founded was to help English sailors.

6. The English rulers knew the value of whatever they did for trade.

7. In 1884, an international conference determined the world's time zones, and imaginary lines called meridians separated the zones.

8. Because the Greenwich Observatory did so much for timekeeping, the starting point for the world's time zones was located there, and this prime meridian is called the Greenwich Meridian.

Lesson 1

The Principal Parts of a Verb

Teaching

Every verb has four principal parts: the **present,** the **present participle,** the **past,** and the **past participle.** With helping verbs, these four parts make all the verb's tenses and forms.

Present	Present Participle	Past	Past Participle
decide	(is) deciding	decided	(has) decided
form	(are) forming	formed	(have) formed
win	(is) winning	won	(has) won

The past and past participle of a **regular verb** are created by adding *–d* or *–ed* to the present. Spelling changes are needed in some words, for example, *hurry—hurried.*

Parts of an **irregular verb** are formed in many ways. These examples show five patterns:

	Present	Past	Past Participle
Group 1 Present, past, and past participle are the same.	let put split spread	let put split spread	(has) let (has) put (has) split (has) spread
Group 2 Past and past participle are the same	bring get lead teach	brought got led taught	(has) brought (has) got *or* gotten (has) led (has) taught
Group 3 Form past participle by adding *-n* or *-en* to past.	beat bear bite choose	beat bore bit chose	(has) beaten (has) borne (has) bitten (has) chosen

	Present	Past	Past Participle
Group 4 Change *i* in the present form to *a* for the past and to *u* for past participle	begin ring sink spring	began rang sank sprang	(has) begun (has) rung (has) sunk (has) sprung
Group 5 Change vowel of present to form past. Add *–n* or *–en* to present to form most past participles.	do fall see write	did fell saw wrote	(has) done (has) fallen (has) seen (has) written

Using Principal Parts of Regular and Irregular Verbs

Complete each sentence by writing the principal part of the verb indicated in parentheses. On the line to the right, write **R** or **I** to indicate whether the verb is regular or irregular.

1. Our class will be _____ (**visit;** present participle) the
   Supreme Court Building. _____

2. During the last term, the court_____ (**split;** past) on several
   major cases. _____

3. The Supreme Court term _____ (**begin;** present) on the first
   Monday each October. _____

4. Although the Court received thousands of petitions for hearings, the Justices have
   _____ (**put;** past participle) less than 100 cases on their schedule. _____

5. The Justices are _____ (**write;** present participle) their opinions
   on the latest case. _____

CHAPTER 4

The Principal Parts of a Verb

Lesson 1

More Practice

A. Writing the Correct Forms of Verbs

Decide which form is needed: the present participle, the past, or the past participle of each verb given in parentheses. Write the correct form on the line.

1. Oliver Wendell Holmes, Jr., (begin) his term on the U.S. Supreme
   Court in 1902.   _____

2. In 1931, when he was 90, Justice Holmes was still (speak)
   words of wisdom.   _____

3. Students today who (choose) to study law will read many of his decisions. _____

4. He never (shrink) from controversy, saying the law must be
   expedient for all.   _____

5. He had (break) with the mainstream so often that he became known as
   the "Great Dissenter."   _____

6. He always (take) his belief that "The life of the law has not been logic:
   it has been experience" into the courtroom.   _____

7. His philosophy of *judicial restraint* (grow) into the dominant way of thinking. _____

8. He had (see) that law should reflect economic and social realities. _____

9. Accordingly, he (write) *The Common Law,* published in 1881, which
   argued that laws should evolve as society changes.   _____

10. He had (wear) the Supreme Court Justice robes for 30 years when
    he died.   _____

B. Using Principal Parts of Regular and Irregular Verbs

Complete each sentence by writing the principal part of the verb indicated in parentheses. On the line to the right, write **R** or **I** to indicate whether the verb is regular or irregular.

1. Those running shoes usually _____ (**cost;** present) an exorbitant price. _____

2. I _____ (**enjoy;** past) the concert even though I was in the last row. _____

3. Jim has _____ (**hurt;** past participle) himself in every game this season. _____

4. The band members were on the field, _____ (**practice;** present
   participle) formations.   _____

5. The footlights were _____ (**shine;** present participle) in the actor's eyes. _____

6. Every balloon used in the pep rally has already _____ (**burst;** past participle). _____

7. I can't talk until I have _____ (**put;** past participle) away the dishes. _____

8. That group of friends has always _____ (**sit;** past participle) in the last
   seat of the bus.   _____

The Principal Parts of a Verb

Application

A. Proofreading for the Correct Forms of Verbs

Draw a line through each incorrect verb form in this paragraph. Draw this proofreading symbol ∧ next to the error and, in the spaces between lines of type, write the correct form of the verb.

> **EXAMPLE** On some cases, a later court has ~~took~~ ∧ *taken* a different position than an earlier court.

The Supreme Court beginned its existence with only five Justices. Initially the Justices also traveled throughout the United States to hear cases. When the country is spreading too far westward, the burden borned by the five judges became too great and Congress added more seats. However, at that time the Court and its rulings were not politically significant. In 1801, the Court ringed in a new era when John Marshall was appointed Chief Justice. In his 34 years as Chief Justice, he is leading the Court to an improved stature within the government. In *Marbury v. Madison*, he announced the doctrine of judicial review, which letted the Court to declare laws unconstitutional. This past century sees the Court make major rulings in the sphere of civil rights. Under Chief Justice Earl Warren, the Court banned racial segregation in public schools in *Brown v. Board of Education.* Currently, the Court's makeup becomes more diverse in the past century with the appointments of the first Jew, first African American, and first woman to the bench.

B. Using Verb Forms Correctly

Write a paragraph that uses at least four of these verbs and verb phrases. Underline each of the verbs and verb phrases. Make sure all verb forms are used correctly.

is/are speaking	will be thinking	has/have heard	agree
will have done	would have told	was/were beginning	took

_____

_____

_____

_____

_____

_____

Verb Tenses

Teaching

Verb tenses indicate when an action or state of being occurs—in the past, present, or future. There are three **simple tenses** and three **perfect tenses**. The set of forms that express the different tenses of a verb is called the **conjugation** of the verb. Below, only the present tense and present perfect tense of *call* are fully conjugated.

Simple Tenses

	Singular	Plural
Present Expresses an action as it happens, or that happens regularly. (May express future or past; see note below.)		
1st Person	I call	we call
2nd Person	you call	you call
3rd Person	he/she/it calls	they call
Past Expresses an action that began and ended in the past.		
3rd Person	he/she/it called	they called
Future Expresses an action that will begin in the future.		
3rd Person	he/she/it will call	they will call

Perfect Tenses

	Singular	Plural
Present Perfect Expresses an action that was completed at an indefinite time in the past, or that started in the past but continues in the present.		
1st Person	I have called	we have called
2nd Person	you have called	you have called
3rd Person	he/she/it has called	they have called
Past Perfect Expresses an action that occurred before another action in the past.		
3rd Person	he/she/it had called	they had called
Future Perfect Expresses an action that will take place before another in the future.		
3rd Person	he/she/it will have called	they will have called

With a modifier indicating future time, the present form expresses a future event *(We meet this evening)*. The **historic** or **literary present tense** describes a past event as if it were happening now *(In the story, the meeting ends in a brawl)*.

Using Verb Tenses

Underline the form of the verb that correctly completes the sentence. On the blank, identify the tense of the verb.

1. The brakeman (broke, has broken) his ankle when he jumped from the train. _____

2. Who (will lead, will have led) the cheers at the game next Friday? _____

3. Three of the candidates (will speak, will have spoken) before the reporters arrive. _____

4. Last year Helen (departed, had departed) for college in a nearby state. _____

5. My parents (resided, have resided) on Ivy Lane since their marriage. _____

6. Hal (sees, has seen) Yo-yo Ma and Itzhak Perlman in concert twice since May. _____

7. Tomorrow I (will go, will have gone) to the pool for my lifesaving course. _____

8. As her opponent watches in dismay, the tennis pro expertly (drops, dropped) a serve just inside the line. _____

9. The car sputtered and then stalled, for it (ran, had run) out of gas. _____

Lesson 2

Verb Tenses

More Practice

A. Using Verb Tenses

Underline the form of the verb that correctly completes the sentence. On the blank, identify the tense of the verb.

1. Tomorrow, we (will have gone, will go) grocery shopping for the party later this week. _____

2. By the time I finish making my grocery list, the store (will have closed, closed) already. _____

3. Denise (had bought, bought) an ice cream cake for me before my sister made me my birthday cake. _____

4. When my grandmother goes shopping, she (used, uses) lots of coupons. _____

5. Since I moved here, I (have gone, had gone) to the supermarket every Thursday. _____

6. My mother (will have bought, had bought) the milk when she realized the expiration date was passed. _____

7. Casey (work, worked) as a bagger at the supermarket while he was in high school. _____

8. The seafood department (sells, has sold) fresh lobster every day so far this summer. _____

9. The bakery was popular because it (gives, gave) free samples to its customers. _____

10. The shopping cart I am using (wobbles, wobbled). _____

B. Correcting Verb Tenses

In each sentence below, correct the error in the underlined verb to show the correct order of events. Write the correct verb form on the line to the right.

1. I already <u>do</u> the dishes by the time she arrived. _____

2. The twins looked and acted alike, even though they <u>will live</u> apart for years. _____

3. The batter <u>swung</u> his bat as the ball whizzes past. _____

4. By the time the tournament is over, we <u>have seen</u> six tennis matches. _____

5. Yesterday Peter <u>will deny</u> all knowledge of the incident. _____

6. "During this term, you <u>have read</u> ten British novels," Mr. Zia predicted. _____

Lesson 2 Verb Tenses

Application

A. Using Verb Tenses

Rewrite the sentence below four ways, changing the tense of its verb to the tense indicated in parentheses. Add phrases or clauses as needed to show correct use of the new verb tense.

Sentence   I bought eight packages of Snack-Eeze at the supermarket.

EXAMPLE   (future perfect) *Before the prices change, I will have bought eight packages of Snack-Eeze at the supermarket.*

1. (present) _____

_____

2. (present perfect) _____

_____

3. (future) _____

_____

4. (past perfect) _____

_____

B. Correcting Verb Tenses

Revise the underlined verbs in the following paragraph to correct errors and show the proper sequence of events. Rewrite the paragraph below.

Before the Great Depression began, Michael Cullen <u>has built</u> the first supermarket in Queens, New York. During the Depression, supermarkets grow because they were a good way to mass-distribute food at low cost. Before cars and refrigerators <u>become</u> common, people <u>will go</u> to small, nearby markets almost every day. Supermarkets <u>grew</u> in size since the 1930s. Most supermarkets now <u>have sold</u> a wide variety of foods, including ready-to-eat meals.

_____

_____

_____

_____

_____

_____

Lesson 3 · Progressive and Emphatic Forms   *Teaching*

The **progressive form** of a verb describes an ongoing action or state of being. Each of the six tenses has a progressive form.

Progressive Tenses		
Tense	Describes an action or state of being . . .	Example
Present	in progress	Rescue teams **are hurrying** to the disaster area.
Past	ongoing in the past	Families **were searching** all day for the missing.
Future	ongoing in the future	The governor **will be touring** the scene soon.
Present Perfect	that started in the past and continues in the present	Volunteers **have been searching** the rubble for survivors.
Past Perfect	interrupted by another past action	Before this tremor, scientists **had been predicting** possible activity along the fault.
Future Perfect	that will take place by a specific future time	By noon, some people **will have been trapped** for a full two days.

The **emphatic form** of a verb (*do* + verb) makes the verb more forceful. This form has only two tenses, present (using *do*) and past (using *did*).

These rescue teams **do seem** more organized than teams in other disasters.

Identifying Verb Tenses

Underline every verb in the progressive form once. Underline any verb in the emphatic form twice. On the line to the right, name the form of each underlined verb.

EXAMPLE Yes, I did say that the earth was shaking for several minutes. *past emph, past prog*

1. The scientists are studying the destruction from the earthquake to determine which buildings are the most earthquake resilient. _____

2. We had been sleeping when we were awoken by the earthquake. _____

3. The reporter has been talking all morning about the damage caused by the quake. _____

4. The principal did say that we will be having an earthquake drill before the end of the week. _____

5. After the hurricane hit the island, the rain was rushing down the hillsides. _____

6. Many people have been living in the streets for the past few days because they were afraid to go back home. _____

7. At the end of the month, the team will have been inspecting the city's buildings for one year. _____

8. The president does want to meet the survivors. _____

9. The tsunami will be hitting the coastline in only a few moments. _____

10. Seismologists are analyzing the data to find out the earthquake's magnitude. _____

Lesson 3 # Progressive and Emphatic Forms   *More Practice*

A. Identifying Verb Tenses

Underline each progressive and emphatic verb form in these sentences. On the
line to the right, name the form of each underlined verb.

1. I did see the movie you were talking about.   _____

2. Before he gave the presentation, the speaker had been reading
   over his notes.   _____

3. By the time my friend gets here, she will have been traveling for
   eight hours.   _____

4. The hikers did take a break after they had been hiking for
   four hours.   _____

5. The television does make the actress appear taller.   _____

6. My boss has been working with the Senator since the election. _____

7. The puppies had been chewing on the shoes before they were
   caught.   _____

8. The leaves will be changing colors during the autumn.   _____

9. Bailey and Nikki have been going to the parade every year.   _____

10. Everyone is eating the chocolate chip cookies Mom made.   _____

B. Using Verb Tenses

Underline the verb form in parentheses that best completes each sentence.

1. Scientists (had researched, have been researching) ways to predict earthquakes.

2. The giant wave (is traveling, will have been traveling) for almost half an hour
   before it strikes.

3. Actually, the islands (did receive, are receiving) a warning of the destructive
   tsunami, but there was little time to get to safety.

4. Clearly the school (will have been instructing, does instruct) their students on
   how to react in an emergency.

5. The emergency supplies of water and food (do arrive, will be arriving) at the
   damage site tomorrow.

6. Due to the landslide, the houses (have been sliding, are sliding) downhill all day.

7. Water pipes (have been remaining, did remain) intact throughout the
   earthquake.

8. In fact, the helicopter crew (did make, was making) some miraculous rescues
   after the landslide.

9. Currently, residents (have been rushing, are rushing) home to find out which
   apartments collapsed.

10. Damage (does appear, is appearing) to be less here than closer to the epicenter.

Lesson 3 Progressive and Emphatic Forms   *Application*

Using Verb Tenses Effectively

The purpose of the following editorial is to condemn lax enforcement of building codes, which caused many apartment buildings to collapse during an earthquake, resulting in many deaths. However, because of an ineffective use of verbs, the editorial does not have a forceful effect. Almost all the verbs are in simple tenses. Rewrite the editorial, combining sentences and using a variety of verb forms, including perfect, progressive, and emphatic forms. Use the facts as presented in the original editorial.

> Last week an earthquake struck our city. Everyone who lives here knows about the danger of quakes in the area. Other earthquakes struck our city before. In the past, large sections of the city were destroyed. When those building went up, nobody knew much about making buildings earthquake-proof. But scientists and engineers researched the problem. They found better building methods. Many homes, offices, and apartment buildings were constructed using the improved methods. Those buildings survived last week's quake. According to law, all contractors should use the improved methods. The government hired inspectors, and the inspectors collected their pay. But did they work? Some buildings that fell down were next to buildings that showed little damage. Why? Look at the materials that lie in the fallen buildings. Even a child can see how flimsy the steel girders are. Where were the inspectors? Why haven't they done their job?

_____

_____

_____

_____

_____

_____

_____

_____

_____

_____

_____

_____

_____

_____

CHAPTER 4

Active and Passive Voice

Teaching

A verb is in the **active voice** when the subject performs the action.

> Aristotle **devised** a system. (The subject *Aristotle* performs the action.)

A verb is in the **passive voice** when the action is received by the subject.

> The system **was devised** by Aristotle. (The subject *system* receives the action.)

The **passive form** may be used only for transitive verbs (verbs that can take direct objects). It combines a form of *be* with the past participle of the main verb. In general, avoid passive voice. However, use it to emphasize the receiver of an action or when the performer of the action is unknown.

Identifying Active and Passive Voice

The main verb in each sentence is in boldface type. If the performer of the action named by that verb is identified, write that word on the line to the right. Also, write **A** if the verb is in active voice or **P** if it is in passive voice.

> **EXAMPLE** Today, plants **are categorized** according to a system developed by a scientist named Linnaeus. *P*

1. Since ancient times, biologists **have recognized** the need for a system of classification for living things. _____

2. The first classification system **was offered** by the Greek philosopher, Aristotle. _____

3. Aristotle **divided** plants into three groups: herbs, shrubs, and trees. _____

4. Animals **were** also **placed** into three groups: land dwellers, water dwellers, and air dwellers. _____

5. This system seems simple to us today because we **have** more information about plants and animals. _____

6. The modern system of classification of plants and animals **is called** *taxonomy*. _____

7. Carolus Linnaeus, a Swedish botanist, **introduced** the modern scientific method of naming plants and animals. _____

8. In this system, every living thing, whether plant or animal, **is given** a name with two parts. _____

9. This system **is called** *binomial nomenclature*, which means "two-name naming." _____

10. Latin and Greek words, because they are understood by scientists in many countries, **are used** in scientific classification. _____

11. Plants and animals **are known** by different common names in different regions. _____

Lesson 4 Active and Passive Voice

More Practice

A. Identifying Active and Passive Voice Verbs

Underline the main verb in each sentence. On the line to the right, label the verb **A** for active voice or **P** for passive voice.

1. People assumed an important role in changing plants about 10,000 years ago. _____

2. Some plants, more than others, were noticed by farmers because of their size. _____

3. With seeds from these plants, farmers hoped to grow bigger plants. _____

4. The basic food crops of the world were developed by this method. _____

5. For example, large cobs with many kernels were produced from tiny ears of corn by the Indians of North and South America. _____

6. Following this pattern of planting seeds from the best plants, farmers have greatly increased the amount of grain produced by rice and wheat. _____

7. Through such methods of plant breeding, scientists have developed plants resistant to disease and insects. _____

8. Luther Burbank, an American plant breeder, experimented with almost 200 groups of plants. _____

9. At his farm, Burbank produced many new vegetables, fruits, and flowers. _____

10. Despite these successes, the breeding of plants is not widely considered an exact science. _____

B. Identifying and Changing the Voice of Verbs

Identify the voice of each verb. Then rewrite each sentence, changing the verb's voice.

> **EXAMPLE** Monthly meetings on gardening are held by the club. *passive*
> *The club holds monthly meetings on gardening.*

1. Carolus Linnaeus was always fascinated by plants. _____

_____

2. In the Netherlands, Linnaeus obtained a medical degree. _____

_____

3. Linnaeus introduced a practical system for classifying plants and animals. _____

_____

4. Careful descriptions of many plants and animals were made by Linnaeus throughout his life. _____

_____

CHAPTER 4

Name _____ Date _____

Lesson 4 · **Active and Passive Voice**   *Application*

A. Revising to Avoid Passive Voice

Revise this paragraph, changing verbs from passive to active voice where appropriate.

> One method of producing a better plant is called hybridization. In
> hybridization, two different plants are crossed. A new, hybrid strain is the
> result. With luck, the desirable traits of its parents will be combined in the
> new hybrid. Many new plants have been developed by this method. When it
> is successful, hybridization produces larger plants, plants that bear more fruit,
> or plants that grow more quickly. Some of the plants that have been created
> by this method are more resistant to disease and unfavorable weather.

_____

_____

_____

_____

_____

_____

_____

B. Using Active and Passive Voice

You are a truck driver hauling a load of bananas. The car in front of you stops
without warning, you hit your brakes, and your load of bananas flies out of the truck
and all over the highway. Write a short report to submit to your company explaining
the accident and its aftermath. Use at least two verbs in active voice and at least
two verbs in passive voice. Make sure that the sentences with passive-voice verbs
are not weak and would not sound better with active-voice verbs.

_____

_____

_____

_____

_____

_____

_____

_____

Lesson 5 · Mood of Verbs

Teaching

The **mood** of a verb indicates the status of the action or condition it describes. There are three moods. **Indicative mood** is used to make statements and to ask questions.

Statement	James Naismith invented the game of basketball in 1891.
Question	Was dribbling legal in basketball's earliest years?

Imperative mood is used to give a command or to make a request. Usually the subject, *you,* is understood and not stated.

Command	Pass the ball to an open player.

Subjunctive mood is used in two situations. It may be used to express a wish or to state a condition that is contrary to fact, or for a command or request following the word *that.*

The subjunctive form of *be* is always *be* or *were,* even with singular subjects.

The player asked that practice *be* held every day.
My brother wishes he *were* taller.
The coach asked *that* the referee explain his call.

A. Identifying the Mood of a Verb

Indicate the mood of each underlined verb by labeling it with **IND** for indicative, **IMP** for imperative, or **SUBJ** for subjunctive.

1. My favorite basketball player of all time, Larry Bird, <u>played</u> in Boston. _____

2. I wish I <u>were</u> as good a player as Bird. _____

3. "<u>Practice</u> every day," my coaches tell me. _____

4. I asked that my parents <u>buy</u> a basketball hoop for the driveway. _____

5. I <u>will attend</u> the same college as Bird did, Indiana State University. _____

6. Bird <u>led</u> his team to three championships. _____

7. The league <u>named</u> Bird their most valuable player three years in a row. _____

8. Every year I say, "<u>Win</u> the national championship again, Boston." _____

9. Prior to his induction, I had urged that Bird <u>be elected</u> to the Hall of Fame. _____

10. Many fans <u>credit</u> Bird with re-creating interest in the game. _____

B. Using Subjunctive Mood

Underline the correct form of each verb in parentheses

1. The EMT ordered that he (put, puts) ice on his ankle that he sprained in the game.
2. The fans wished the punter (was, were) able to kick a little further.
3. The team requests that the game (be, was) postponed because of rain.
4. The coach recommended that the players (rely, relied) on each other.
5. The players demanded that the referee (stops, stop) favoring the other team.

Mood of Verbs

More Practice

A. Identifying Moods of Verb

Identify the mood of the underlined verb in each numbered item. On the corresponding line below, write **Indicative, Imperative,** or **Subjunctive.**

(1) The girls' soccer games at the university <u>are</u> very exciting. (2) The players ask that every fan <u>wear</u> only blue and white, the school colors. (3) This year, the team wants to win the championship. <u>Wish</u> them luck! (4) Last year the team <u>advanced</u> to the semifinals but lost after their goalie was injured. (5) If she <u>remains</u> healthy all season, the team believes they will win. (6) To achieve this goal, the coach demands the players <u>be</u> at practice every day for three hours. (7) <u>Tell</u> the coach to make sure his players work on their footwork. (8) Fans enjoy games when the players <u>make</u> tricky moves. (9) Last year's star forward <u>holds</u> the record for the most goals scored in a season. But she has already graduated. (10) I wish she <u>were</u> still on the team to break more records.

1. _____

2. _____

3. _____

4. _____

5. _____

6. _____

7. _____

8. _____

9. _____

10. _____

B. Using the Correct Mood of a Verb

Underline the correct form of the verb. On the line to the right, indicate which mood you used. Write **IND** for indicative, **IMP** for imperative, or **SUBJ** for subjunctive mood

1. The student wishes that he (was, were) able to play beach volleyball year round. _____

2. "(Run, Runs) down the field," shouted the coach to his forwards. _____

3. The referee demands that the ice hockey player (return, returns) to the penalty box. _____

4. James (join, joins) an Ultimate Frisbee team wherever he lives. _____

5. The golfer asked that the fans (are, be) silent during the tournament. _____

6. Unless every player on the opposing basketball team (was, were) suddenly able to float, we knew we had this game won after the first period. _____

Lesson 5

Mood of Verbs

Application

A. Proofreading for Correct Mood

The following letter to a newspaper uses the indicative mood for almost every verb. Revise the passage to include at least five verbs in the imperative mood or subjunctive mood.

> The professional checkers players are going on strike again. They are on strike because they want a raise from the checkers league owners. The players already make enough money. Everyone should tell them that. The public wishes to see the players jump opponents' pieces and crown kings again. I want the players to stop their strike and to play the game again. If I played checkers professionally, I would talk sense into the other players on my team. If the owners listened to my recommendations, I would tell them to be strict with the players.

_____

_____

_____

_____

_____

_____

_____

B. Using the Correct Mood

Write one or two paragraphs about your favorite sports team or player. Include in your passage at least two verbs in the indicative mood, at least two in the imperative mood, and at least two in the subjunctive mood.

_____

_____

_____

_____

_____

_____

_____

_____

CHAPTER 4

Name _____ Date _____

Lesson 6

Problems with Verbs

Teaching

Misusing Tenses Avoid misusing tenses by following these rules:

Use the same tense to express two or more actions that occur at the same time.

  While the crowd **watched** breathlessly, the trapeze artists **presented** their act.

To show a sequence of past events, use the past perfect or past progressive tense to describe the oldest event and the simple past to describe the most recent one.

  After the entire cast **had paraded** into the tent, the circus **began.**

Confusing Verbs Avoid using the wrong verb in these pairs of similar verbs:

Verb	Definition	Example
lie, (is) lying, lay, (has) lain	to rest in a flat position	The tiger lay in the ring.
lay, (is) laying, laid, (has) laid	to place	The tamer laid down his whip.
rise, (is) rising, rose, (has) risen	to go upward	Balloons rose to the roof.
raise, (is) raising, raised, (has) raised	to lift	Workers raised the tent.
sit, (is) sitting, sat, (has) sat	to occupy a seat	The audience sat on risers.
set, (is) setting, set, (has) set	to put or place	Who set this box in the aisle?
leave, (is) leaving, left, (has) left	to go away from	The magician left in flash.
let, (is) letting, let, (has) let	to allow	He let a fan keep his hat.

Avoiding Problems with Verbs

Underline the correct verb in parentheses.

1. Before we bought tickets to the circus, we (saw, had seen) advertising for it.
2. My little brother begged my parents to (leave, let) him go with me.
3. As soon as we found our seats and (sat, set) down, the ringmaster appeared.
4. He (rose, raised) his top hat in a salute to the audience.
5. We (laughed, had laughed) as the clowns performed their tricks.
6. After a tiny car had been driven into the ring, we (marveled, had marveled) as a dozen clowns piled out.
7. In one act, elephants (stand, stood) on their hind legs and danced.
8. Later, a trainer (sat, set) a series of hoops in the ring, and her dogs jumped through every one.
9. The jugglers (lay, laid) down their clubs before they started tossing a set of flaming torches back and forth.
10. Trained horses cantered in a circle while riders (jumped, have jumped) from horse to horse.
11. Some circus acts (are, were) dangerous, and performers risk their lives daily.
12. It was a tense moment when the lion refused to obey a command, but the fierce animal finally (lay, laid) down.
13. The whole audience (rose, raised) to their feet when the high-wire act ended.
14. As we (left, let), the sights and sounds of the circus remained with us.

Lesson 6 Problems with Verbs

More Practice

A. Correcting Misused Tenses and Confused Verbs

Underline any error in verb usage in the following sentences. Write the proper verb on the line. If all verb forms in a sentence are correct, write **Correct.**

1. The antique car had set in the garage unused for 40 years.

   _____

2. Ancient fossils have been discovered laying in creek beds.

   _____

3. Hundreds of people have dined at the restaurant where we have eaten yesterday.

   _____

4. Although food costs are raising, my salary has not increased.

   _____

5. He should have left us borrow his CDs for the party.

   _____

6. The defendant rose his left hand while being sworn in.

   _____

7. Ann sings along as she listens to music.

   _____

8. When Molly sits the dough in a warm place, it will rise.

   _____

9. I had thought about the election for a long time before I decided how to vote.

   _____

10. Lay that aside and help me with the groceries, please.

    _____

11. Stop offering advice and left us finish the job alone.

    _____

12. After she stood in line for an hour, she finally reached the ticket counter. _____

B. Correcting Misused Tenses

Six sentences in this passage contain incorrectly used verbs. On the lines below, write the numbers of the sentences with errors, and the correct forms of the misused verbs.

   (1) The world-famous magician stepped onto the stage. **(2)** First, he sat a board between two chairs with the ends of the board resting on the backs of the chairs. **(3)** Then, he asked for a volunteer from the audience. **(4)** The volunteer, a young girl, laid down on the board.
   (5) The magician waved his wand and the girl suddenly started raising. **(6)** The magician passed a hoop around the girl hanging in mid-air. **(7)** He left the audience see there were no strings attached. **(8)** Next, he motioned with his wand and the volunteer slowly descended. **(9)** The girl landed gently on the board and set up, looking rather dazed. **(10)** The magician thanked the girl and left the stage while the audience had applauded.

_____   _____

_____   _____

_____   _____

Name _____ Date _____

Problems with Verbs

Application

A. Correcting Verb Errors

Rewrite each sentence to correct any errors in verb forms. If the tenses and verb choice need no correction, write **Correct.**

1. Many American poets have lived abroad, and they benefit from exposure to foreign cultures.

   _____

2. John Tagliabue drew the ideas for many of his poems from the travel journals that he kept whenever he visits such exotic places as Peru, Syria, Nepal, and China.

   _____

   _____

3. Similarly, when Allen Ginsberg lived in India in the 1960s, he, too, kept travel journals, which he had later used as source material for poems.

   _____

   _____

4. A poet who does not travel must use familiar images in fresh ways.

   _____

   _____

B. Using Verbs Correctly

Write one or two paragraphs describing a live show you have seen. Use at least five of the verbs listed below in your description. Make sure that the tenses you use accurately reflect the order of events.

    lie   lay   raise   rise   set   sit   leave   let

_____

_____

_____

_____

_____

_____

_____

_____

_____

Name _____ Date _____

Agreement in Person and Number

Teaching

A verb must agree with its subject in number. Singular subjects take singular verbs; plural subjects take plural verbs. The form of a verb must also agree with the person of its subject. Except for the verb *be,* the only form that changes is third person, singular present.

	Verbs Other than Be		Be, Present Tense		Be, Past Tense	
	Singular	**Plural**	**Singular**	**Plural**	**Singular**	**Plural**
1st	I dance	we dance	I am	we are	I was	we were
2nd	you dance	you dance	you are	you are	you were	you were
3rd	he/she/it dances	they dance	he/she/it is	they are	he/she/it was	they were

Don't be distracted by other words separating the subject and verb.

The **girl** in the tap shoes **has danced** since she was six.

A. Identifying Subjects and Verbs That Agree in Number

In each sentence, underline the subject and the verb. On the line to the right of the sentence, write whether the two parts of the sentence **Agree** or **Disagree** in number.

1. Ballet dancers train for many years. _____

2. Those tap shoes on the shelf is a size too small for me. _____

3. The costume with the bright spangles was reflecting light from the stage. _____

4. The dancers in Ms. Lewis's class is practicing for a holiday program. _____

5. Near the end of the *pas de deux,* the man tosses the woman into the air. _____

B. Making Subjects and Verbs Agree in Number

In each sentence, circle the verb in parentheses that agrees with the subject.

1. The St. Louis flag (show, shows) two wavy bars and a *fleur-de-lis.*

2. Many masks worn at this party (cost, costs) a great deal.

3. I (was, were) sure that our float would be the best in the parade.

4. Motorists in England (drive, drives) on the left-hand side of the road.

5. Over one million people (visit, visits) the monument annually.

6. The last two albums by that singer (has, have) gone platinum.

7. The crown jewels of England (are, is) kept in the sublevel of the Tower of London.

8. Caliban, one of Shakespeare's fantastic characters, (is, are) a revolting monster.

9. You (was, were) the best speaker in the debate on Friday.

10. One person standing before the 4,000 patrons (sing, sings) the anthem.

11. Cahokia Mounds State Park (call, calls) to mind Native American settlements.

12. Those tests (was, were) the hardest ones so far this year.

Agreement in Person and Number

More Practice

A. Making Subjects and Verbs Agree in Number

On the line to the right of each sentence, write the present tense form of the verb in parentheses that agrees with the subject.

1. Several buildings of historical interest (lie) in or near the downtown area. _____

2. That route past the fallen trees (be) closed during clean-up. _____

3. Many plays by Shakespeare (take) place in Italian towns. _____

4. Tropical plants (grow) in the greenhouse attached to the garden center. _____

5. This memorial (honor) the men and women who served in World War I. _____

6. The girls on Jan's team (be) determined to win the competition next week. _____

7. Every tourist, along with residents, (enjoy) the sight of the Louvre. _____

8. I (be) ready to read my essay to the class now. _____

9. The London Underground, a system of subway rails, (transport) millions of riders. _____

10. You (be) the only one in our class competing in the obstacle course. _____

B. Correcting Agreement Errors

Underline the six verbs in this paragraph that do not agree with their subjects. On the lines below, write the numbers of the sentences in which you find agreement errors. After each sentence number, write the subject and the correct verb form.

(1) Don't laugh. I, along with several teammates, are in the dance program next week. (2) Our coach, of all people, is responsible. (3) Dancers of any quality has great muscle tone, he says. (4) Apparently this fan of forward passes appreciate dance as well as sports. (5) Anyway, the arts department has scheduled this show. (6) Posters all over the school asks for volunteers. (7) My buddies on the team have friends in a dance class. (8) One of their friends have taught us a simple dance. (9) The dancers from our team practices every night. (10) We know our coach is in for a surprise.

_____   _____

_____   _____

_____   _____

Agreement in Person and Number

Lesson 1

Application

A. Proofreading for Errors in Agreement

Find the verbs in this paragraph that do not agree with their subjects. On the lines below, rewrite the paragraph, correcting all agreement errors.

> Probably the most popular ballet in the United States is *The Nutcracker*. In some cities, the local ballet company, at the request of many patrons, perform this ballet every year through the winter holidays. Many families in town has a tradition of seeing the ballet annually. Small parts in the performance is played by children from the area. The story of the ballet, like that of many other tales, tell of a dream. At a Christmas party, a little girl receives the gift of a nutcracker in the form of a bold soldier. That night, the nutcracker appears in the girl's dream. Fantastic characters in the dream dances to beautiful music by Peter Tchaikovsky.

_____

_____

_____

_____

_____

_____

B. Making Subjects and Verb Agree in Writing

Choose one of the topics below and write a paragraph of at least five sentences about it. Use the present tense throughout. Make sure the subjects and verbs of all the sentences agree.

The Best Dancers I Know   Why I Like (or Dislike) Ballet

Famous Dancers   The Best Dance Scene(s) in Movies

a popular dance of past or present (Charleston, twist, break dancing, etc.)

an ethnic dance (the polka, Irish step dancing, the hora, African dance, etc.)

_____

_____

_____

_____

_____

_____

CHAPTER 5

Name _____   Date _____

Indefinite Pronouns as Subjects   *Teaching*

Some **indefinite pronouns** are always singular. Examples are *each, everyone, neither, nobody, another, anybody, anyone,* and *something.* They take singular verbs.

> <u>Each</u> of the playgoers **has** a favorite play by Shakespeare.

Some indefinite pronouns, including *several, few, both,* and *many,* are always plural. They take plural verbs.

> <u>Many</u> at tonight's play **agree** that this performance was special.

Some indefinite pronouns, including *some, all, most,* and *none,* are singular or plural depending on how they are used.

> <u>Most</u> of the <u>actors</u> **were** outstanding. (There are many actors.)

> <u>Most</u> of the <u>publicity</u> **was** accurate. (The publicity is considered as one quantity.)

A. Identifying Indefinite Pronouns

In each sentence, underline the indefinite pronoun used as the subject and the verb. On the line, label the subject **Singular** or **Plural.** If the pronoun can be either singular or plural, draw two lines under the word naming the person(s) or thing(s) it refers to.

> **EXAMPLE** <u>Some</u> of the <u>music</u> was written for this performance. *Singular*
> <u>Some</u> of the <u>songs</u> were from Shakespeare's time *Plural*

1. Nobody among the actors is nationally known.   _____

2. All of the evening flies past.   _____

3. Several of the critics are in the audience.   _____

4. Some of the scenery stands out in your memory.   _____

5. Most of the famous speeches sound fresh and new.   _____

6. None of the other current plays outshine this one.   _____

B. Making Indefinite Pronouns and Verbs Agree

In each sentence, underline the indefinite pronoun used as the subject. Then circle the verb form in parentheses that agrees with the subject.

1. Few of the trees (has, have) leaves anymore.

2. Although Toni bumped the table, none of the soup (was, were) spilled.

3. Everyone at the stores (is, are) in a holiday mood.

4. Nothing in these boxes (look, looks) like my lost sweater.

5. Most of the cars in this lot (is, are) sport utility vehicles.

6. Anybody on the staff (substitute, substitutes) in emergencies.

7. Either of the twins (know, knows) where to find the key.

8. All of her theories (seem, seems) to be stolen from this book.

9. Several of the songs on the album (has, have) an exotic Oriental sound.

10. Some of the baby's toys (amuse, amuses) his parents, too.

Indefinite Pronouns as Subjects

More Practice

A. Making Verbs Agree with Indefinite Pronoun Subjects

In each sentence, underline the indefinite pronoun used as the subject. Also underline the verb. If the verb agrees with the subject, write **Correct** in the blank. If it does not agree, write the correct verb in the blank.

1. Something in those leftovers have an unpleasant odor. _____

2. Many of our traffic lights are still out. _____

3. Neither of the chairs appear very strong. _____

4. All of the stones in the wall was quarried locally. _____

5. Several of the accessories was included in the package price. _____

6. Nobody on their team help each other. _____

7. Most of the soil in those containers come from Mr. Doohan's garden. _____

8. Everybody in line for tickets has an umbrella. _____

9. None of our worry were needed. _____

10. Both of the possible dates for the picnic is in August. _____

11. Most of Steve's neighbors tolerate his bugle practice gracefully. _____

12. All of the spokespeople for the city agrees on the need for street repairs. _____

B. Using Verbs with Indefinite Pronoun Subjects

Write each numbered sentence on the appropriate line, using the correct present tense form of the verb.

The final scenes of *Romeo and Juliet* move quickly. **(1)** Few of the characters (know) that Romeo and Juliet are secretly married. **(2)** Everything (fall) apart after Juliet drinks the sleeping potion. Romeo should be told that she is merely sleeping. **(3)** None of the message (get) delivered. **(4)** Because of this mistake, both of the "star-crossed lovers" (commit) suicide. **(5)** All of the Veronese people (mourn) with the reconciled Capulet and Montague families.

1. _____

2. _____

3. _____

4. _____

5. _____

Name _____ Date _____

Lesson 2 Indefinite Pronouns as Subjects   *Application*

A. Checking Agreement of Verbs with Indefinite Pronoun Subjects

Proofread this paragraph for errors in subject-verb agreement. Underline any verb that does not agree with its subject.

In William Shakespeare's *Romeo and Juliet,* no one knows the origin of the feud between the Montagues and Capulets. Many of the citizens in Verona has participated in the feud. At the Capulets' masked ball, everyone understand that the prince will punish any who fight. None of the guests is disruptive. Some of the Montagues attends in costume. Nobody else holds the interest of Juliet after this youngest one of the Capulets meet Romeo at the party. In turn, nothing but loving thoughts are on Romeo's mind after that meeting. But in the course of the play, all of the young lovers' plans end in tragedy.

B. Using Verbs Correctly with Indefinite Pronouns as Subjects

Think of a play you have seen about which you can write a paragraph. Use at least five of these phrases as subjects of sentences. You may use the phrases in any order, and may write additional sentences with different subjects as well. Write your paragraph on the lines below. Make sure each verb is in the present tense and agrees with its subject.

Somebody in the cast   All of the audience members

Both of the scenes   Many of them

None of it   Some of the action

_____

_____

_____

_____

_____

_____

_____

_____

_____

_____

Lesson 3

Compound Subjects

Teaching

A **compound subject** is made up of two or more subjects joined by a conjunction.

A compound subject whose subjects are joined by *and* usually requires a plural verb.

> Ham, eggs, *and* juice **are** in the refrigerator.

However, compound subjects that function as a single unit take singular verbs. Also, compound subjects preceded by *each*, *every*, or *many* take singular verbs.

> Ham and eggs **is** a popular breakfast.

> Every adult and child **needs** a nutritious breakfast.

When the parts of a compound subject are joined by *or* or *nor*, the verb should agree with the part closest to it.

> **Is** the ham *or* the eggs in the oven? Either the ham *or* the eggs **are** there.

Making Verbs Agree with Compound Subjects

In each sentence, first decide whether the compound subject is a special case. **(1)** Do the two parts function as one unit? Or does *each*, *every*, or *many* appear before the compound subject? Then underline both parts and the connecting word with one line. **(2)** If neither of these situations is true, underline each part of the compound subject separately and underline twice the word joining the parts. Finally, underline the correct verb.

> **EXAMPLES** Each school club and sports team (has, have) its own set of rules.
> Neither the bees nor their queen (want, wants) to leave the tree.

1. Every spring and fall (see, sees) me cleaning out my closet to make more space.
2. Neither Friday night nor weekend afternoons (was, were) open on Don's schedule.
3. Either my uncle or his children (has, have) planned to bring a barbecue grill.
4. That tree or those bushes (hold, holds) the robin's nest.
5. Many a young man and woman (is, are) surprised by the SAT vocabulary test.
6. One boy or two girls at the school (has, have) a chance for that scholarship.
7. Neither Viola nor her brothers (like, likes) turnips.
8. Rhythm and blues (is, are) my favorite type of music.
9. Certain elements and combinations of elements (is, are) called minerals.
10. The students and teachers in the room (has, have) a real interest in the speakers.
11. Neither Marcus nor Cara (has, have) spoken before a large group before.
12. Each clock and watch in the store (is, are) reset for Daylight-Saving Time.
13. Either the highway or the side streets (provide, provides) a fast route to the theater.
14. My cousins or my sister (borrow, borrows) my camera every month.
15. The flowers and the ferns (was, were) arranged in a vase.
16. Either the phone connections or the modem itself (cause, causes) the computer to crash whenever I go online.

Lesson 3

Compound Subjects

More Practice

A. Using the Correct Verb with a Compound Subject

Write the correct form of the verb in parentheses. Make it agree with the compound subject.

1. Either my grandparents or my cousins (have) time to watch my game.   _____

2. Next week or those two weeks (suit) me best for a vacation.   _____

3. Neither the students nor their teacher (want) to miss the trip because
of snow.   _____

4. Spaghetti and meatballs (take) very little effort to prepare.   _____

5. Those sparrows or that chickadee (eat) most of the seed in our feeder.   _____

6. Each knob and handle (catch) my sweater as I walk through the kitchen.   _____

7. The groceries and the laundry (be) still in the car.   _____

8. The Rumford Medal in physics and the Emerson Thoreau Medal in
literature (be) given by the American Academy of Arts and Science.   _____

9. Each junior and senior (have) a voice in the recommendation.   _____

10. The electrician or the custodians (be) going to repair the clock.   _____

11. Rock and roll (have) been popular for half a century.   _____

12. Neither the horn nor the brake lights on that car (work).   _____

B. Correcting Errors in Agreement

Find the mistakes in the paragraph. For each sentence, write the correct present
tense verb to agree with the subject. If the verb does agree, write **Correct.**

     (1) Very bright light and very dim light are both perceived by the human
eye. **(2)** Neither the eye nor the other sense organs is invulnerable. **(3)** Care
and appropriate caution is necessary for healthy eyes. **(4)** Every child, athlete,
and other active adult need unbreakable plastic lenses in eyeglasses. **(5)** Either
goggles or a protective shield in front of the eyes are recommended for
workers exposed to hazardous materials. **(6)** Welders, carpenters, painters,
and chemists have to exercise good judgment in caring for their eyes.

1. _____   **4.** _____

2. _____   **5.** _____

3. _____   **6.** _____

Name _____ Date _____

Compound Subjects   *Application*

A. Combining Sentences Using Compound Subjects

Rewrite the following paragraph, combining sentences where possible by using
compound subjects. Use *and, or, nor, either . . . or,* or *neither . . . nor* to join the
parts of the subject. Keep the action in the tense of the two original sentences that
are joined.

     Dad often goes fishing. I often go along. We bring home a bucket of fish.
Every little fish smells. Every big fish has an odor, too. So Dad does not like to
cook fish. Mom does not like doing that, either. Therefore, my sisters and I
have learned to cook fish dishes. Fish with rice is a satisfying meal. Or fish
and chips makes a good meal. How did we learn to cook? Books have been
helpful. CD-ROMs have been good, too. So have cooking shows on TV. Now
everyone in the family, except Dad, can cook. However, my sisters do not
clean the fish. Mom does not clean the fish. Can you guess who gets stuck
with that job?

_____

_____

_____

_____

_____

_____

_____

B. Using the Correct Verb with Compound Subjects

Think of a skill you have learned to do on your own. Write a paragraph explaining
what you learned, how you did so, and why. Use at least one example of each of
these: a compound subject whose parts are joined by *and;* a compound subject
whose parts are joined by *or* that takes a singular verb; and a compound subject
whose parts are joined by *or* that takes a plural verb.

_____

_____

_____

_____

_____

_____

CHAPTER 5

Other Confusing Subjects

Teaching

A **collective noun** names a group of people or things. Examples include *team*, *family*, *committee*, *jury*, and *herd.* When the members act as a unit, the collective noun takes a singular verb. When they act as individuals, it takes a plural verb.

> The <u>herd</u> **is** valuable. (seen as one)
>
> The <u>herd</u> **are** in their stalls. (seen separately)

Phrases or clauses that serve as subjects of sentences always take singular verbs.

> <u>That family farms are disappearing</u> **is** a sad truth. <u>To deny it</u> **is** useless.

Some nouns ending in *–s* appear to be plural but are singular in meaning and therefore take a singular verb. Examples include *mumps, mathematics, news*, and *molasses.* Other nouns ending in *–s*, such as *pants*, take plural verbs even though they name one thing.

> Simple <u>mathematics</u> **proves** the difficulty of farming profitably.

Numerical amounts and titles of works of art, literature, or music are considered singular. Fractional numbers are singular only if they refer to a singular noun.

> <u>The Farmers</u> **is** a painting at the museum. <u>Two-thirds</u> of it **shows** equipment.

When a relative pronoun is the subject of an adjective clause, it agrees in number with its antecedent. Relative pronoun subjects include *who, which, what*, and *that.*

> Heavy debt is one of the <u>problems</u> <u>that</u> **drive** farmers into giving up. (*That*
>
> refers to *problems*, so it takes a plural verb.)

Using Verbs That Agree with Problem Subjects

In each sentence, underline the subject and the form of the verb that agrees with it. If the subject is a relative pronoun or a fractional number, underline twice the word it refers to.

1. Numismatics (is, are) the study of coins and medals.
2. The cast (is, are) changing their costumes during intermission.
3. How the magician got out of the locked safe (puzzle, puzzles) us.
4. My scissors (is, are) made for left-handed people.
5. Two-thirds of a gallon (is, are) enough to paint the whole room.
6. Dr. Chian is a surgeon who (specialize, specializes) in reconstructive surgery.
7. To wait for some Web sites to download (challenge, challenges) the patience of every Web surfer.
8. *Pictures at an Exhibition,* an orchestral work, (was, were) inspired by actual paintings seen by the composer at an exhibition.
9. Our team (has, have) the best record in the league.
10. Listening to loud music for long periods (cause, causes) hearing loss.
11. Two hours (seem, seems) a long time to wait to see the doctor.
12. This article was written by two reporters who (was, were) recently hired.
13. (Is, Are) the binoculars in the case?

Other Confusing Subjects

Lesson 4

More Practice

A. Using Verbs That Agree with Problem Subjects

In each sentence, underline the verb that agrees in number with the subject. If the subject is a relative pronoun or a fractional number, underline twice the word it refers to.

1. The TV news (start, starts) at half past the hour.
2. Over 30 hours (is, are) required for the hike up the mountain.
3. How well (do, does) your sewing scissors cut heavyweight corduroy?
4. Whether a replacement switch (is, are) available is not yet known.
5. *Belles on Their Toes* (is, are) still a funny book, even if it is dated.
6. A panel of experts (is, are) going to decide the question.
7. One-fifth of that pie (belong, belongs) to me.
8. Mentioning old cars to my grandfather always (set, sets) off reminiscences.
9. The family (disagree, disagrees) on where they should spend the holidays.
10. Mr. Southard is one of the teachers who (insist, insists) on conferences.

B. Writing Sentences

Complete each of these sentences by adding a present-tense verb as described in the parentheses, and any other needed words.

EXAMPLE (plural verb) Three-fourths *of these diskettes are already full.* _____

1. (singular verb) The women's choir _____

_____

2. (plural verb) The women's choir _____

_____

3. (plural verb) Two-thirds _____

_____

4. (singular verb) Two-thirds _____

_____

5. (singular verb) The work crew _____

_____

6. (plural verb) The work crew _____

_____

Other Confusing Subjects

Application

Lesson 4

A. Proofreading for Subject-Verb Agreement

Proofread this paragraph for errors in subject-verb agreement. Draw a line through each incorrect verb. Then draw this proofreading symbol ∧ next to the word and write the correction above the error.

One of the biggest difficulties that makes redecorating a long process is planning. First, do the family agree on what is to be done? If only one-half the members wants a new color in the kitchen, how much the job costs don't enter the debate. Once the family comes to an agreement, determining the necessary materials come next. When measuring for wallpaper, remember: ten square yards are not the same as 30 square feet. To estimate costs is usually the next step. Mathematics are important now, as you compare costs of possible purchases. For example, every paint can and varnish can have information about coverage of its product. Are three gallons of a particular paint enough or too much? Making the final choices and scheduling the work is the last hurdles.

B. Using Confusing Subjects Correctly in Writing

Outline the plot of a mystery, or describe a single scene of a mystery. Use each of the phrases below as the subjects of sentences as indicated. In addition, use at least one noun clause as a subject.

The team of detectives (use with singular verb)
The team of detectives (use with plural verb)
This act is one of those crimes that (use to begin a complex sentence)

The pliers (or The scissors)
A thousand dollars

_____

_____

_____

_____

_____

_____

_____

_____

_____

CHAPTER 5

Special Agreement Problems

Lesson 5

Teaching

The form of some sentences can make identifying the correct verb difficult.

In an **inverted sentence,** the subject follows the verb or part of the verb. Reordering the words in the standard order can help you find the subject and the verb.

Question:	**Does** your <u>school</u> **offer** courses in keyboarding?
	Your <u>school</u> **does offer** courses in keyboarding.
Beginning phrase:	With every era **comes** new <u>technology</u>.
	New <u>technology</u> **comes** with every era.

An **imperative sentence** may not state the subject; it is almost always *you.*

<u>(You)</u> **Imagine** having to make your own pencils!

In almost every **sentence beginning with *here* or *there,*** the subject follows the verb.

There **are** <u>inkwells</u> in the desks in the school display at the museum.

In a sentence with a **predicate nominative,** the verb must agree with the subject, not the predicate nominative.

<u>Inkblots</u> on their papers **were** a constant problem for students of the 1800s.
A constant <u>problem</u> for students of the 1800s **was** inkblots on their papers.

Solving Agreement Problems

In each sentence, underline the subject if it is stated. Then circle the correct verb.

1. There (lie, lies) your new box of red pens.
2. How (does, do) Joshua maintain high grades and play baseball at the same time?
3. Handwriting errors (is, are) a thing of the past with computers.
4. Another technological aid (is, are) spell-checker programs.
5. On the door of the computer room (hang, hangs) schedules for different classes.
6. Here (is, are) the notes for my history paper
7. Tomorrow (buy, buys) enough paper for this term.
8. (Does, Do) any stores in this area sell fine fountain pens?
9. Even in a high-tech school, pencil sharpeners (is, are) a necessity.
10. Out of the printer (shoot, shoots) one page after another.
11. (Is, Are) this computer available during the next hour?
12. There (is, are) a huge pile of books left in the computer room.
13. According to novelists, ribbons ruined by being dunked in inkwells (was, were) a daily problem for schoolgirls in the past.
14. Why (has, have) you waited till the last minute to start writing your paper?
15. In the next aisle (is, are) cartridges for inkjet printers.

CHAPTER 5

Name _____ Date _____

Special Agreement Problems

More Practice

A. Solving Agreement Problems

In each sentence, find and underline the subject if it is stated. Then write the present tense form of the verb that agrees with the subject.

1. Why (be) *Beowulf* one of the most famous epic poems? _____

2. There (go) our last chance for the pennant! _____

3. After the meal, (store) the tables in the storage space under the stage. _____

4. Out of the opening in the earth (rise) the volcanic vapors. _____

5. The problem with this car (be) the brakes. _____

6. Why (have) so many earthquakes occurred in that area? _____

7. There (stand) the first building erected in this town. _____

8. Entire orchards (be) the result of Johnny Appleseed's efforts. _____

9. After each Sunday football game (come) the Monday morning quarterbacking. _____

10. Here (come) the two most beautiful floats in the entire parade. _____

B. Correcting Agreement Errors

Find the four sentences in this paragraph in which the verb does not agree with the subject. On the lines below, write the numbers of those sentences and the correct verb forms.

(1) One of the latest advances in technology for students are computers. **(2)** There are some colleges that require students to use computers for assignments. **(3)** Not long ago, typewriters and the ballpoint pen was the highest level of technology. **(4)** Does your parents remember doing homework with noneraseable ink? **(5)** Many times, a student wrote and rewrote compositions many times because of tiny handwriting errors. **(6)** Greatly appreciated was teachers who accepted papers in pencil. **(7)** If you use a computer and printer for your writing assignments, appreciate technology!

_____   _____

_____   _____

Special Agreement Problems

Lesson 5

Application

A. Using Sentence Variety and Agreement

Combine one or more of the subjects listed below with one of the verbs to write a sentence in which the subject follows the verb or part of the verb. The verbs may be used in the active or passive voice and in one of these tenses: present, present progressive, present perfect, or present perfect progressive. Create five sentences.

Subjects: pencil(s)   eraser(s)   student(s)   teacher(s)
              parent(s)   computer(s)   fountain pen(s)   ballpoint pen(s)

Verbs: be   use   buy   work   serve   like

1. _____

2. _____

3. _____

4. _____

5. _____

B. Revising for Sentence Variety and Agreement

The goal of this writer was to experiment with unusual sentence order. The effect is difficult to read. In addition, several of the sentences have errors in subject-verb agreement. Revise the paragraph to sound more natural by using standard subject-word order in a few of the sentences. Remember to make all verbs agree with their subjects and keep verbs in the present tense. Use an additional piece of paper if necessary.

Gone is the days when ink pens blotted compositions! From my grandmother comes this report of her first term paper. In the library sits she, taking notes. Snaps her pencil lead. Around the stacks roam she in search of a pencil sharpener. There is books listed in the card catalogue that are not on the shelves. Broken pencils and missing books is only a part of her problem. Finally finished is her outline. Produced next is seven incomplete handwritten versions of the paper. Greatly relieved is she when turned in are the final version.

_____

_____

_____

_____

_____

_____

CHAPTER 5

Nominative and Objective Cases

Lesson 1

Teaching

Personal pronouns change their forms, called **cases,** depending on how they function in a sentence. The three cases are nominative, objective, and possessive.

		Nominative	Objective	Possessive
Singular	***First Person***	I	me	my, mine
	Second Person	you	you	your, yours
	Third Person	he, she, it	him, her, it	his, her, hers, its
Plural	***First Person***	we	us	our, ours
	Second Person	you	you	your, yours
	Third Person	they	them	their, theirs

Use the **nominative case** of a personal pronoun when the pronoun functions as a subject or a predicate nominative, or as part of a compound subject.

Subject   I have been learning about President Eisenhower.
Part of compound subject My grandmother and I were talking about the 1950s.

A **predicate pronoun** takes the nominative case. It immediately follows a linking verb and identifies the subject of the sentence.

Predicate pronoun   The president elected in 1953 was he.

Use the objective case of a personal pronoun when the pronoun functions as a direct object, indirect object, or object of a preposition. Use it also when the pronoun is part of a compound object.

Direct object   The Republicans nominated <u>him</u> for president.
Indirect object   People voting in 1952 gave <u>him</u> 55 percent of the vote.

Object of preposition   My grandmother campaigned for <u>him</u>.
Part of compound object   Voters decided between Adlai Stevenson and <u>them</u>.

To decide which case to use in a compound construction, consider each part separately.

A. Identifying the Case of a Pronoun

Identify the case of each boldfaced personal pronoun in the following sentences. On the line write **N** for nominative or **O** for objective.

1. Dwight Eisenhower was born in Texas, but **he** grew up in Kansas.   _____

2. Classmates nicknamed his big brother "Big Ike" and gave **him** the name "Little Ike."   _____

3. Both his brother and **he** raised and sold vegetables.   _____

B. Using the Correct Case of Personal Pronouns

Underline the correct pronoun to complete each sentence.

1. During World War II, (he, him) commanded the Allies' military forces.
2. The decision to launch D-Day was difficult for his advisors and (he, him).
3. After the war, the first commander of NATO forces was (he, him).

Lesson 1

Nominative and Objective Cases

More Practice

A. Using the Correct Case of Personal Pronouns

In each sentence, underline the correct pronoun form.

1. Dwight Eisenhower became president in 1953; voters re-elected (he, him) in 1956.

2. Everybody called (he, him) Ike, so his campaign buttons read "I Like Ike."

3. The public first learned about (he, him) as an Army general during World War II.

4. His friend General George Patton and (he, him) were both heroes of the war.

5. By the end of the war, the general in charge of all Allied forces was (he, him).

6. As supreme commander of the Allied forces, Eisenhower selected reliable people for his staff and depended on (they, them) to carry out their responsibilities.

7. As president, he selected people he trusted for his cabinet so that he and (they, them) could work well together.

8. He created the Department of Health, Education, and Welfare and appointed Oveta Culp Hobby to head (it, they).

9. That action made (she, her) a member of Eisenhower's cabinet.

10. The other cabinet members and (she, her) had to be strong managers.

11. Eisenhower's vice-president, Richard Nixon, succeeded (he, him) as president.

12. His wife Mamie and (he, him) retired to their farm in Gettysburg, Pennsylvania.

B. Choosing Personal Pronouns

Fill in the blanks in the following sentences with appropriate personal pronouns. Vary the person and number of the pronouns, and do not use the pronoun *you*.

1. Joel and _____ hope to get tickets for the opening day of the auto show.

2. Kendra invited T.J. and _____ to come over and watch a movie.

3. Cassie will go with Vinnie and _____ to the museum exhibit next week.

4. Will Cho and _____ play a duet for the recital?

5. Gymnastics is what Margo and _____ plan to take next fall.

6. The fans gave Tracy and _____ a standing ovation for their dance program.

7. Was it Langston Hughes or _____ who wrote the poem called "Dreams"?

8. The flute players in our orchestra will be Mr. Kruse and _____.

9. The widower, who had one daughter, divided his estate equally among

    _____ and her brothers.

10. No one thought the owner of the sports car to be _____.

CHAPTER 6

Nominative and Objective Cases

Lesson 1

Application

A. Proofreading

Proofread the following story to make sure that the correct cases of pronouns have been used. When you find a pronoun used incorrectly, cross it out. Then insert this proofreading symbol ∧ and write the correct pronoun above it.

During Dwight Eisenhower's first term, one of the most dangerous people in the country was Senator Joseph McCarthy of Wisconsin. McCarthy had gained national attention in 1950 by claiming that there were Communist spies in the government. His Senate subcommittee and him held televised hearings. TV viewers watched McCarthy's allies and he as they charged individuals with being Communist sympathizers. People were afraid to fight McCarthy because their friends and them would be called Communists too. McCarthy tried to ban books as well. He said them and their authors supported Communists. President Eisenhower made it clear there was a difference of opinion between him and McCarthy. In 1953, the President was making a speech to Dartmouth College students. He told they and their teachers, "Don't join the book burners." McCarthy continued to attack people and give them problems with getting and keeping jobs. But him and his allies never produced proof. Finally, in December of 1954, the rest of the Senate condemned him and they. That move stopped his threat.

B. Using Personal Pronouns in Writing

Write a paragraph about a recent president whom you admire, or a person you believe would make a good president. Be sure to use personal pronouns correctly.

_____

_____

_____

_____

_____

_____

_____

_____

Lesson 2 # Possessive Case   *Teaching*

Personal pronouns that show ownership or relationships are in the **possessive case.**

> The possessive pronouns *mine, ours, yours, his, hers, its,* and *theirs* can be used in place of a noun. These pronouns can function as subjects or objects.

> We won't mix up our black jackets. <u>Mine</u> has red buttons; yours has white ones.

> The possessive pronouns *my, our, your, his, her, its,* and *their* can be used to modify a noun or a gerund. The pronoun precedes the noun or gerund it modifies. Do not use a possessive pronoun with a participle.

> <u>Our</u> buying similar clothes has given us problems. (*buying* used as gerund)

> My aunt saw <u>us</u> buying boots yesterday. (*buying* used as participle)

Don't confuse these possessive pronouns with the contractions that they sound like: *their/they're (they are), its/it's (it is), your/you're (you are).*

A. Identifying Possessive Pronouns

Underline all the possessive pronouns in each sentence.

1. My brother and I share a room, but his things are always on my desk and my bed.
2. My clothes are hung up, but his are all over, including on top of mine.
3. He had books stacked so high that their weight broke a shelf.
4. Mom borrowed my camera because she had lost hers, and she took pictures of her room and ours.
5. Do other people have problems with their siblings like the ones I have with mine?

B. Using Personal Pronouns Correctly

In each sentence, underline the correct pronoun form.

1. The cast appreciated (him, his) hard work helping them learn their parts.
2. The plates with the blue rim are (our, ours).
3. Please turn off that alarm before (its, it's) buzzing deafens me.
4. (Me, My) worrying about the test did not affect the result.
5. Olga took her skates home, but she left (your, yours) on the bench.
6. Many of the kindergartners had trouble putting on (they're, their) boots.
7. Haddonfield, New Jersey's claim to fame is (it, its) being the site of the first dinosaur skeleton discovered in North America.
8. Joan heard (him, his) singing the Broadway tunes at the benefit performance.
9. Has the deadline for applications passed, or may Leah still turn (her, hers) in?
10. (Your, You're) interrupting our song spoiled the recording.
11. The coach didn't object to (them, their) being late for practice.
12. The tree cast (it's, its) shadow on the picnic table.
13. I need to borrow an umbrella because I left (my, mine) at the library.
14. We found the cat in (its, it's) usual hiding place.
15. He couldn't understand (me, my) walking out in the middle of a fine rehearsal.

Name _____ Date _____

A. Using Personal Pronouns Correctly

In each sentence, underline the correct pronoun form.

1. The doctor praised (them, their) exercising on a rowing machine at least three times a week.

2. Why is the rubber plant losing (its, it's) leaves?

3. (Him, His) devising an identification certificate for refugees earned the Norwegian explorer Fridtjof Nansen the Nobel Peace Prize in 1922.

4. You shouldn't be taking (your, you're) time to do someone else's job.

5. (Them, Their) making the first successful powered airplane flight guaranteed the Wright brothers a place in history.

6. The whole team watches (them, their) practicing for the mixed doubles championship match.

7. Have all the students found (they're, their) seats?

8. That biology book is either (yours, your) or mine.

9. I was awakened by (you, your) banging on the screen door.

10. A shark's skin is abrasive because of (it, its) having toothlike scales.

11. Aren't you amazed at (us, our) being able to remember all those dates?

12. I tried to picture (you, your) wearing a helmet and carrying a spear in an opera.

B. Using Personal Pronouns Correctly

Fill in the blanks in the following sentences with appropriate possessive pronouns.

1. Every family has _____ problems.

2. Two brothers or two sisters will share _____ clothes and then argue about who got the clothes torn.

3. A toddler sees her brother's toy and, even though she has her own, she wants _____ too.

4. Older children bring _____ problems from school home with them.

5. As if there weren't enough problems at home already, parents bring _____ from their jobs.

6. Usually my mother can keep _____ temper when things

   go wrong, but I always lose _____.

7. My family and I don't believe that _____ is an unusual home.

8. I'm asking you for _____ thinking on the matter.

Lesson 2 # Possessive Case   *Application*

A. Proofreading for Pronoun Errors

Proofread the following essay. When you find a possessive pronoun used incorrectly, cross it out. Then insert this proofreading symbol ∧ and write the correct pronoun above it.

     Sometimes, when I have an argument with mine family, I compare ours problems with those of other families. You should try it. When you look at the difficulties that characters in Greek tragedies have with they're relatives, you're family will look wonderful.

     For example, there was Oedipus. The parents of baby Oedipus tried to kill him. Them hearing a warning that he would kill his father and marry his mother drove them to it. But when they left they're child outside to die, he was saved and grew to manhood. Him not knowing who he was resulted in tragedy when he fulfilled the prophecy.

     And think about Electra. While Electra's father was off at war, hers mother took a lover. Electra longed to see her father, but upon him coming home, Mom and her lover killed him. To Electra, no crime was worse than their. She waited till her baby brother grew up and then helped him kill they're mother and hers lover.

     No matter how upset I get at home, me knowing what Electra's family was like makes mine attractive. For yours sake, I hope that the same is true of you're situation.

B. Using Pronoun Cases Correctly in Writing

Write a paragraph about a time when you or someone else in your family had a problem with other members of the family, and how the problem was resolved or came to an end. Use the correct cases of personal pronouns in your sentences. Be sure to use at least five pronouns in the possessive case. Use a separate piece of paper, if necessary.

_____

_____

_____

_____

_____

CHAPTER 6

Lesson 3 *Who* and *Whom*   *Teaching*

The case of the pronoun *who* is determined by the pronoun's function in the sentence.

Nominative	who, whoever
Objective	whom, whomever
Possessive	whose, whosever

Who and *whom* can be used to ask questions and to introduce subordinate clauses.

In a question, who is used as subject or predicate pronoun. The objective pronoun *whom* is used as a direct or indirect object of a verb or as the object of a preposition.

Subject   <u>Who</u> will be the new principal?
Indirect object   <u>Whom</u> did you tell about the rumor?
Object (of preposition) From <u>whom</u> did you hear the news?

When deciding whether to use *who* or *whom* in a subordinate clause, consider only how the pronoun functions in the clause. If it is the subject, use *who*. If the pronoun is an object in the subordinate clause, use *whom*.

Subject of clause   The person <u>who</u> replaces Ms. Theo has to be good.
Object in clause   The students <u>whom</u> Ms. Theo supervised will miss her.

Using *Who* and *Whom* Correctly

In each sentence, underline the correct pronoun form. If the pronoun choice is in a subordinate clause, first draw brackets [ ] around the clause, and then mark the right choice.

   EXAMPLE When will we know [(<u>who</u>, whom) will get the job]?

1. Everyone in school wonders (who, whom) our new principal will be.
2. No one knows (who, whom) actually chooses the person for the job.
3. We certainly hope that he or she will give the job to (whoever, whomever) seems best qualified.
4. Our present principal, (who, whom) everyone likes and respects, has held the position for 15 years.
5. To (who, whom) has Ms. Theo explained her reasons for leaving?
6. Mr. Capp, (who, whom) is the assistant principal, says that Ms. Theo is retiring.
7. From (who, whom) did he hear that?
8. Mr. Capp didn't say from (who, whom) he heard his information.
9. Could the person (who, whom) replaces Ms. Theo be someone at school now?
10. Probably it can be anyone (who, whom) is qualified, perhaps even Mr. Capp.
11. (Who, Whom) could we ask for more information?
12. My mother knows someone (who, whom) is on the school board.
13. Her friend might not give information to just anyone (who, whom) asks.

Who and *Whom*

A. Identifying the Function of *Who* and *Whom*

In the following sentences, determine the function of *who/whoever or whom/whomever.* If a sentence uses *who* or *whoever,* underline once the verb of which it is the subject. If a sentence uses *whom* or *whomever,* underline twice the verb or preposition of which it is an object.

> **EXAMPLES** People **who** <u>gossip</u> should find better things to do.
>
> Some gossips talk about **whomever** they <u>choose</u>.

1. **Whom** is Richard inviting to the prom?
2. We argued about **who** the hero really was.
3. The ad offers a reward to **whoever** returns the missing wallet.
4. **Whom** do you think the voters will elect?
5. The very proper butler inquired, "May I ask **who** is calling?"
6. Is Captain Ahab the character **who** pursued the white whale Moby Dick?
7. To **whom** did the judges award first prize?
8. The reporters were misinformed about **whom** the governor had named to the post.
9. Leave the message with **whoever** answers the phone.
10. Can you tell **whom** Harry is imitating?

B. Using *Who* and *Whom* Correctly

In each sentence, underline the correct pronoun form.

1. Does anyone know (who, whom) took the photo of the chorus?
2. The prize will go to (whoever, whomever) deserves it.
3. Toby asked him (who, whom) the book was for.
4. Amos, (who, whom) called last night, is working at Fred's gas station.
5. No one in the cabin knew (who, whom) our new counselor was.
6. Arlene, (who, whom) is fluent in Spanish, won the scholarship to Spain.
7. Mrs. Judson is a teacher (who, whom) everyone admires.
8. The team will accept (whoever, whomever) the coach chooses.
9. We were surprised when we discovered (who, whom) the salesclerk was.
10. The singer (who, whom) no one could hear, seemed nervous.

Lesson 3

Who and *Whom*

Application

A. Proofreading for *Who* and *Whom*

Proofread the following paragraph. Decide whether each numbered use of some form of *who* is correct. If the wrong form of the pronoun is used, write the correct form on the line below. If the correct form is used, write **Correct.**

Norman Rockwell was a painter **(1)** whose work usually presented stories of everyday happenings. The people **(2)** who he presented were average-looking, the sort of person **(3)** who you might meet on the street. **(4)** Whoever saw his illustrations on the cover of the *Saturday Evening Post* recognized easily **(5)** whomever appeared there. For example, one memorable illustration is named *The Gossips.* The illustration is made up of 15 tiny scenes. In each, two people are talking, either face-to-face or by phone. The woman **(6)** who appears at the top left, beginning a rumor, also appears at the bottom right, hearing with dismay the effects of what she started. In between are the people **(7)** whom hear and pass on the rumor. Even if the ages and the hairstyles of the characters **(8)** who you see in the illustration may not match those of the gossips you know, you recognize in the work the attitudes of **(9)** whomever indulges in gossip.

1. _____
2. _____
3. _____

4. _____
5. _____
6. _____

7. _____
8. _____
9. _____

B. Using *Who, Whom,* and *Whose* in Writing

Rewrite each sentence or pair of sentences below as a single sentence that uses a subordinate clause introduced by or containing *who, whom,* or *whose.* Use the pronoun given in parentheses in your new sentence.

EXAMPLE I will skate with that girl. She just began taking lessons. (who)
I will skate with the girl who just began taking lessons.

1. George Washington was a leader. He was respected even by his enemies. (who)

_____

2. Mrs. Tarleton called the mother of the boy. His application came in late. (whose)

_____

3. Many a boy and girl entered the contest. Each one of them won a prize. (whoever)

_____

4. Here is the phone number of the counselor. You wanted to call her. (whom)

_____

5. Min contacted many people for support in the election. She impressed all of them. (whomever)

_____

Pronoun-Antecedent Agreement

Teaching

A pronoun must agree with its antecedent in number, gender, and person. An **antecedent** is the noun or pronoun that a pronoun refers to or replaces.

If the antecedent is singular, use a singular pronoun. If it is plural, use a plural pronoun.

> Because this <u>dollhouse</u> is almost 300 years old, <u>it</u> is historically important.

> The <u>furnishings</u> are noticeably different from <u>their</u> modern counterparts.

Compound Subjects A plural pronoun is used to refer to nouns or pronouns joined by *and.*

> The tiny <u>chest</u> and <u>dresser</u> still have <u>their</u> original hardware.

A pronoun that refers to nouns or pronouns joined by *or* or *nor* should agree with the noun or pronoun nearest to it.

> Neither the bedrooms nor the <u>dining room</u> have <u>its</u> original drapery.

With Collective Nouns A collective noun such as *class* may be referred to by either a singular or a plural pronoun, depending upon the meaning of the noun in the sentence.

> The <u>family</u> that owns the house loaned <u>its</u> treasure to the library. (singular)

> The <u>family</u> wanted <u>their</u> friends to see the house. (plural)

Gender and Person The **gender** of the pronoun—masculine (*he, his, him*), feminine (*she, her, hers*), or neuter (*it, its*)—must be the same as the gender of its antecedent. The **person** (*first, second, third*) of the pronoun also must agree with the person of its antecedent.

> <u>Any miniaturist</u> would like <u>his</u> or <u>her</u> creation to last for hundreds of years.

> <u>You</u> would be proud to see <u>your</u> work appreciated by future generations.

Identifying Pronouns and Their Antecedents

In each sentence underline once the personal pronoun and underline twice its antecedent.

1. As a child, Aunt Livia often played with her dollhouse.

2. In the 1500s, dollhouse owners used the dollhouses to show off their wealth.

3. The dollhouses were made to imitate their owners' homes.

4. In one place, a rich woman could show visitors how beautifully her whole house was decorated.

5. The man of the house could give guests an idea of treasures he kept in storage.

6. These houses were not small; some of them were six feet high.

7. Dutch merchants made their dollhouses much smaller.

8. The Utrecht Dollhouse, one of the most famous of its kind, consists of a cabinet with tiny furnished rooms instead of drawers or shelves.

9. Craftspeople of the late 1600s gave their talents to creating the Utrecht Dollhouse.

Lesson 4 **Pronoun-Antecedent Agreement**   *More Practice*

A. Identifying Pronouns and Their Antecedents

In each sentence draw an arrow to connect each pronoun with its antecedent.

1. Anyone thinking that dollhouses are only for children should revise his or her belief.

2. Dollhouses of the 1500s and 1600s, miniature copies of their wealthy owners' homes, can help a researcher improve his or her understanding of those times.

3. In the 1920s, a society woman created a dollhouse, and Carrie Stettheimer's artist friends contributed their talents to making it special.

4. Among those friends was the painter Marcel Duchamp, best known for his pioneering the artistic movement called Dada.

5. Duchamp contributed to the Stettheimer dollhouse a tiny work painted by him.

B. Making Pronouns and Antecedents Agree

Underline the pronoun that correctly completes each sentence. Also underline the antecedent(s) of the pronoun.

1. When the team scored a touchdown, the crowd threw (its, their) hats in the air.

2. Neither Carmen nor her sisters have bought a gift for (her, their) brother.

3. Scuba divers are taught that (you, they) should check (your, their) equipment.

4. Patrick and Warren will present (his, their) routine before the other gymnasts do.

5. Not one hiker would set out without (his or her, their) compass.

6. Sal and Marcus shop for clothes here because (you, they) can find good bargains.

7. Either Debbie or Melinda will bring (her, their) ice skates.

8. Anyone who wants a job should bring (his or her, their) application to me.

9. Arctic explorers discover that (you, they) cannot expose skin to the icy air.

10. I told everyone in the boys' choir that (you, he) had to bring a boxed lunch.

11. Neither Carl nor Mark asked (his, their) parents to chaperone the dance.

12. The town council will be presenting (its, their) own proposal for the new park.

13. Fran always liked walking home because (you, she) saved money on bus fare.

14. If (you, they) should fall, experienced in-line skaters know that knee and elbow pads will reduce the risk of injury.

15. Neither Kate nor Anne has had (her, their) vacation pictures developed yet.

Lesson 4

Pronoun-Antecedent Agreement

Application

A. Making Pronouns and Antecedents Agree in Writing

Read the following paragraph. Look especially for errors in agreement between pronouns and their antecedents. On the lines below, write the numbers of the sentences with agreement errors. Then write each of those sentences correctly.

> **(1)** Kathy has always liked dollhouses, and she got an idea for a business from their hobby. **(2)** Now she and her brothers make dollhouses for sale. **(3)** Neither she nor her brothers give all of her time to the business. **(4)** Still, the team makes all its spending money from their sales. **(5)** Kathy's older brother, Murray, builds the shells. **(6)** He chooses the plywood, cuts it to scale, and assembles the pieces. **(7)** Her younger brother, Max, paints the houses inside and out, giving it details like doors, windows, and shutters.
> **(8)** While Murray and Max do his jobs, Kathy buys miniature furniture. **(9)** Then she sews curtains, rugs, tablecloths, and bedspreads to make each house special. **(10)** From October until mid-December, the crew take turns selling its products at craft sales.

_____

_____

_____

_____

_____

_____

_____

_____

B. Writing with Pronouns

Write a description of someone from whom you have learned a craft or how to make something useful. Describe how this person taught you and what you learned. Be sure to include at least five personal pronouns with clear antecedents. Use a separate piece of paper, if necessary.

_____

_____

_____

_____

CHAPTER 6

Lesson 5

Indefinite Pronouns as Antecedents

Teaching

When an indefinite pronoun is the antecedent of a personal pronoun, the personal pronoun must agree in number with the indefinite pronoun. This chart shows the number of some common indefinite pronouns.

Indefinite Pronouns						
Always Singular				**Always Plural**	**Singular or Plural**	
another	each	everything	one	both	all	none
anybody	either	neither	somebody	few	any	some
anyone	everybody	nobody	someone	many	most	
anything	everyone	no one		several		

Use a singular pronoun to refer to a singular indefinite pronoun. The phrase "his or her" is considered a singular pronoun.

> <u>Each</u> of the cars has <u>its</u> sponsor's name painted on <u>it</u>. (singular)

Use a plural pronoun to refer to a plural indefinite pronoun.

> <u>Many</u> of the cars are in <u>their</u> first race. (plural)

Some indefinite pronouns can be singular or plural. Use the meaning of the sentence to determine whether the indefinite pronoun is singular or plural.

> <u>Some</u> of the equipment was still packed in <u>its</u> containers. (singular)

> <u>Some</u> of the race teams were still looking for <u>their</u> equipment. (plural)

Using Indefinite Pronouns

In each sentence, underline the correct pronoun. Also underline its antecedent. If ifs antecedent is a pronoun that can be either singular or plural, underline twice the word that indicates its number in the sentence.

> **EXAMPLE** <u>None</u> of the <u>cars</u> in the race have had (its, <u>their</u>) tires changed.

1. All of the mineral water has lost (its, their) sparkle.
2. Everyone must bring (his or her, their) own instrument to the music class.
3. Last spring one of the baby robins fell and broke (its, their) wings.
4. Nobody appreciates (his or her, their) own good health until illness strikes.
5. None of the books are in (its, their) proper positions on the shelves.
6. Each of the boys enjoyed (his, their) trip to the Art Institute.
7. Both of the girls had to take medication for (her, their) allergies.
8. Each of the exhibits at the museum required (its, their) own special lighting.
9. One of the brochures has a photograph of Barcelona on (its, their) cover.
10. Few of the members on the girls' team had arranged (her, their) own transportation.
11. Everything in the jewelry case has (its, their) own price tag.
12. None of the new dimes have been removed from (its, their) wrapper.
13. Either of those girls may be invited to display (her, their) paintings at the fair.

Lesson 5

Indefinite Pronouns as Antecedents

More Practice

A. Identifying Indefinite Pronouns

Underline the indefinite pronoun in each sentence. Then underline the correct pronoun in parentheses.

1. Each of the baby girls has already received (her, their) vaccinations.
2. Neither of those dogs ever learned to obey (its, their) master.
3. During the violent thunderstorm, most of the county lost (its, their) electricity.
4. All but one of the alligators that escaped from the zoo found (its, their) way back safely.
5. Each of the boys on the team is wearing (his, their) new uniform.
6. Many have expressed (his or her, their) support for our plan.
7. Neither of the women has told me (her, their) opinion.
8. Everyone in the gardens planted (his or her, their) tomatoes just before the unexpected frost.
9. None of the women skaters has taken (her, their) turn on the ice yet.
10. Most of the bus drivers had completed (his or her, their) routes by midnight.
11. Some of the flowers have lost (its, their) fragrance.
12. Several of the men insist that (his, their) votes were not counted.

B. Using Pronouns Correctly

In each sentence below, decide whether the pronouns agree with their antecedents. If the sentence is correct, write **Correct** on the line. If it contains a pronoun that does not agree with its antecedent, rewrite the sentence correctly on the line.

1. None of the spectators at this car race regret his or her attendance.

_____

2. Many of the fans cheered loudly for their favorite drivers.

_____

3. Everybody in the crowd enjoyed their experience here.

_____

4. Do any of the food kiosks have veggie burgers on its menus?

_____

5. Some of the drink that I spilled left its mark on my souvenir booklet.

_____

6. All of the contestants expressed its interest in returning next year.

_____

CHAPTER 6

Lesson 5 | Indefinite Pronouns as Antecedents

Application

A. Proofreading for Pronoun-Antecedent Errors

Proofread the following paragraph. When you find an error involving a pronoun and its agreement with its antecedent, cross the pronoun out. Then insert this proofreading symbol ∧ and write the correct pronoun or pronouns above it. If necessary, mark any verb that must agree with the changed pronoun to be changed, also.

One of the most popular sports worldwide holds their events in stadiums, on city streets, and on mountain roads. That sport is auto racing. Many of the drivers are professionals who earn his or her living from competing. Tens of thousands more, however, are amateurs who participate at their own expense. There are many kinds of auto races, and almost anyone can test their abilities in one of them. For example, some of the drivers in kart races have only celebrated his or her eighth birthday. However, most of the people interested in racing get their pleasure from watching others race. Almost everybody in the United States has heard of drag racing, even if they haven't seen it. Several of the other well known races are known by its French name, Grand Prix, which means "large prize." All of these races draw hundreds of thousands of spectators to its courses on roads in Canada, the United States, Monaco, and other countries.

B. Using Indefinite Pronouns in Writing

Write a paragraph about the sport you most enjoy watching, either live or on television. Explain what makes the event of interest to you. Use at least four of these indefinite pronouns: *all, any, most, none, some.* Be sure that any personal pronouns agree with their indefinite pronoun antecedents in number.

_____

_____

_____

_____

_____

_____

_____

Other Pronoun Problems

Lesson 6

Teaching

Pronouns may be used with an appositive, in an appositive, or in a comparison. Pronouns can also be used reflexively or intensively

Appositives An **appositive** is a noun or pronoun that follows another noun or pronoun to identify or explain it. The pronouns *we* and *us* are often followed by appositives. To determine whether to use *we* or *us,* drop the appositive from the sentence and determine whether the pronoun is a subject or an object.

> <u>We</u> hikers scheduled a ten-mile hike. (<u>We</u> scheduled a ten-mile hike.)
> The park rangers encouraged <u>us</u> hikers. (The park rangers encouraged <u>us</u>.)

A pronoun used in an appositive is in the same case as the noun to which it refers.

> The hike leaders, Kurt and <u>she</u>, planned the route. (*Leaders* is the subject of *planned;* use the nominative case.)
> Club members followed the hike leaders, Kurt and <u>her</u>. (*Leaders* is the object of *asked;* use the objective case.)

Comparisons A comparison can be made using *than* or *as* to begin a clause. When words are left out of such a clause, the clause is said to be **elliptical.** To determine the correct pronoun to use in an elliptical clause, mentally fill in the unstated words.

> My sister likes hiking more than <u>I</u>. (more than I like hiking)
> My sister likes hiking more than <u>me</u>. (more than she likes me)

Reflexive and Intensive Pronouns Pronouns ending in *-self* or *-selves* can be used reflexively or intensively. Reflexive and intensive pronouns may never be used alone; they must refer to, or intensify, an antecedent in the same sentence.

> I <u>myself</u> suggested hiking past Strawberry Lake. (used as intensive pronoun)
> I saw <u>myself</u> in the water of Strawberry Lake. (used as reflexive pronoun)

A. Choosing the Correct Pronoun

In each sentence, underline the correct pronoun form.

1. (We, Us) hikers met at dawn.
2. Ben walked faster than (I, me).
3. The bear chased the two hikers, Lucinda and (he, him), when they approached the cub.
4. The bees stung Barbara fewer times than (I, me).
5. A sudden rainstorm gave (we, us) hikers a slippery path.
6. The slowest walkers, Briana and (she, her), arrived half an hour after the rest of us.
7. (We, Us) survivors decided we'd had a good time.

B. Choosing the Correct Pronoun

In each set, underline the correct sentence.

1. Kendra asked myself a question. / Kendra asked me a question.
2. I myself will help you. / Myself will help you.
3. Kelvin asked himself a question. / Kelvin asked him, Kelvin, a question.
4. Did herself break Tina's lens? / Did Tina herself break her lens?

Other Pronoun Problems

More Practice

A. Choosing the Correct Pronoun

In each sentence, underline the correct pronoun form.

1. Dad handed rakes to both of (we, us) boys.

2. (We, Us) able-bodied rakers attacked the back yard.

3. Lester has longer arms than (I, me).

4. He raked in wide circles around (himself, hisself).

5. (Myself, I myself) preferred to rake one long row at a time.

6. No other pair of rakers could have cleaned off that yard faster than (us, we).

7. (We, Us) workers wanted to get the lawn clear of leaves before any more fell.

8. Unfortunately, the leaves were faster than (we, us).

9. By the time the two of (we, us) boys worked our way across the lawn, the first half was already re-covered with leaves.

10. Later, Dad came to help his sons with sore arms, Lester and (I, me).

B. Using Pronouns Correctly

Write an appropriate pronoun on the line in each sentence. Do not use the pronoun *you* or any possessive pronoun.

1. The two winning gymnasts, Briana and _____, received medals.

2. The administration will not give _____ students a voice in school policy.

3. Marco knows how to play bridge better than _____.

4. Francine was curious about where _____ magicians learn our tricks.

5. _____ latecomers had to wait at the back of the hall till the orchestra finished the first piece.

6. The critics praised several of the artists, especially Wolf Kahn and _____.

7. The blown spray wet me as much as _____.

8. At soccer, Carlos protects the cage better than _____.

9. _____ poets should get together to share ideas and our poems, as well.

10. Izaak is as interested in developing a new cartoon character as _____.

Other Pronoun Problems   *Application*

A. Writing Elliptical Sentences Using Pronouns

Write an elliptical sentence with the same meaning as each of the following
sentences. Replace the boldfaced noun with a pronoun. Use the correct pronoun to
communicate your meaning.

> **EXAMPLE** George is generally more truthful than **Bill** is.
> *George is generally more truthful than **he**.*

1. Anne has been seen on stage by more people than **Emma** has been seen by.

_____

2. Frank is a better driver than **Cher** is.

_____

3. Victor knows as many people in town as **Art** knows.

_____

4. The Wicked Queen was determined to be more beautiful than **Snow White** was.

_____

5. Did you arrive earlier than **Janine** arrived?

_____

6. Nancy is as eager to see Mark as **Becca** is eager to see him.

_____

B. Proofreading for Correct Pronoun Usage

Proofread the following paragraph. When you find a pronoun used incorrectly, cross it
out. Then insert this proofreading symbol ∧ and write the correct pronoun above it.

> To we visitors to Rocky Creek Park, there's no greater challenge than
> climbing Mount Baldy. Two regular park visitors, my neighbor Tom and me,
> tried to scale that smooth cliff again last week. The park rangers warned
> climbers, other teens and we, to stay with buddies. Tom is more daring than
> me, so I keep him in line. I myself need some of his self-confidence. He
> started up faster than me, and for a while I felt bad that I wasn't doing as well
> as him. But then he slowed down. Finally he stopped altogether. He told
> myself that some dirt or dust had gotten into his eyes. He could feel for
> handholds, but he himself couldn't see where to reach over the vertical cracks
> in the wall. We were closer to the top than to the bottom by then, so we
> continued up. But from that point on, I had to see for him as well as for
> myself. No one was more relieved to reach the top than us! Now Tom goes
> around bragging that he can scale Mount Baldy blindfolded.

Name _____ Date _____

Lesson 7 Pronoun-Reference Problems   *Teaching*

If readers cannot find or determine the antecedent of a pronoun, they can be confused.

General reference problems occur when the pronouns *it, this, that, which,* and *such* are used to refer to a general idea rather than to a specific noun. Correct the problem by adding a clear antecedent or by rewriting the sentence to eliminate the pronoun.

Awkward Norse mythology reflects the weather in Scandinavia, which is well known.

Revised It is well-known that Norse mythology reflects the weather in Scandinavia.

Indefinite reference occurs when the pronoun *it, you,* or *they* does not refer to a specific person or thing. Correct the problem by rewriting the sentence to eliminate the pronoun.

Awkward In Norse myths about creation, you have land of ice and mist.

Revised A land of ice and mist appears in Norse myths about creation.

Ambiguous reference occurs when a pronoun could refer to two or more antecedents. Correct the problem by rewriting the sentence to clarify what the pronoun refers to.

Awkward Thor and Odin are two Norse gods; his weapon is the hammer.

Revised Thor and Odin are two Norse gods; Thor's weapon is the hammer.

Identifying Clear Pronoun References

In each pair of sentences below, one sentence has an indefinite, general, or ambiguous pronoun reference. The other is correct. Underline the one that is correct.

1. Thor was Odin's oldest son and the god of thunder and lightning; he was proud of him.

   Thor was Odin's oldest son and the god of thunder and lightning; Odin was proud of him.

2. When Thor threw his hammer, which was magic, it never missed its mark.

   When Thor threw his hammer, it never missed its mark, which was magic.

3. In different Norse myths, you have different versions of certain events.

   Different Norse myths give different versions of some events.

4. Many tales tell of Thor's fantastic appetite.

   It said in many tales that Thor had a fantastic appetite.

5. Thor tried to drink the oceans, which caused the first tides.

   Thor's attempt to drink the oceans caused the first tides.

6. Thor had many battles with giants, the enemies of the gods, and they always came out in his favor.

   Thor had many battles with giants, the enemies of the gods, and those battles always came out in his favor.

Lesson 7

Pronoun-Reference Problems

More Practice

Avoiding Indefinite, General, and Ambiguous References

Rewrite the following sentences to correct indefinite, general, and ambiguous pronoun references. More than one interpretation may be possible. Add any words that are needed to make the meaning clear.

1. According to Norse myths, the gods created the first humans from trees, which makes them odd ancestors. _____

   _____

2. In Greek myths, the home of the gods was the top of Mount Olympus, but in Norse myths you have Asgard. _____

   _____

3. Greek myths told about the Fates and the similar Norns appeared in Norse myths; they lived at the base of the tree that supported creation. _____

   _____

4. In the myths it explains that the three Norns controlled the past, present, and future.

   _____

5. Valhalla was a special place in Asgard, the Norse heaven, for warriors killed in battle, and that gave Viking warriors more courage. _____

   _____

6. The Vikings honored such gods as Odin and Thor; they gave us the names of some weekdays. _____

   _____

7. Odin asked to drink from the spring of wisdom, but it cost him one eye.

   _____

8. In these northern myths they have a god of agriculture called Frey.

   _____

9. The people of ancient times carried an image of Frey with them when they traveled, which they thought would keep them safe. _____

   _____

10. The evil god Loki was jealous of the Balder, the god of beauty, and when he wasn't expecting danger, he killed him. _____

    _____

Lesson 7

Pronoun-Reference Problems

Application

A. Eliminating Pronoun Reference Problem

Revise the sentences below to correct all indefinite, general, or ambiguous pronoun reference problems. More than one interpretation may be possible.

1. Browsing in bookstores is satisfying when you finally find one.

_____

2. Please explain to me what they mean by "Pyrrhic" victory.

_____

3. The difference between an alligator and a crocodile is not important when it is

about to bite you. _____

_____

4. He dropped his headphones, which interrupted the tape.

_____

5. Smitty argued with Dad about the curfew, which made Dad storm out of the room.

_____

B. Using Clear Pronoun References

In the following paragraph, find five sentences with indefinite, general, or ambiguous pronoun references. Revise the sentences on the lines below. Use a separate piece of paper, if necessary.

> **(1)** In Norse myths it talks about gods and giants, magic plants and weapons. **(2)** Two of them were Loki and Balder. **(3)** Loki was an evil god, who hated the other gods, especially Balder. **(4)** Balder, the god of beauty, goodness, and light, was a son of the goddess Frigg and the ruler of the gods, Odin. **(5)** He is also called Woden, and Wednesday is named after him. **(6)** Frigg persuaded all things on earth, even stones, to promise not to hurt Balder, which made Balder lose all sense of danger. **(7)** Nobody but Loki knew that the mistletoe had not made the promise. **(8)** For fun, the blind god Hoder was going to throw something at Balder. **(9)** He gave him a sprig of it to throw. **(10)** The mistletoe pierced Balder's body, killing him.

_____

_____

_____

_____

_____

Lesson 1 # Using Adjectives and Adverbs

Teaching

Modifiers are words that describe, or restrict, the meanings of other words.
Adjectives modify nouns and pronouns. They answer the questions *which one* (that, this), *what kind* (yellow, bright), *how many* (many, few), or *how much* (some, more).

Words classified as other parts of speech can be used as adjectives.

Articles	<u>an</u> event, <u>a</u> dream, <u>the</u> joke
Nouns	<u>snow</u> shovel, <u>sour</u> pickle
Participles	<u>falling</u> snow, <u>frozen</u> river
Possessive nouns and pronouns	<u>Jewell's</u> dress, <u>my</u> mittens
Demonstrative pronouns	<u>that</u> cloud, <u>this</u> poem, <u>these</u> cups, <u>those</u> desks
Indefinite pronouns	<u>every</u> house, <u>any</u> object
Numbers	<u>two</u>, <u>15</u>

Adverbs modify verbs, adjectives, and other adverbs. They answer the questions *when, where, how,* or *to what extent.*

When?	A snowstorm is coming **tomorrow.**
Where?	Bring the flowers **inside.**
How?	The snow fell **gently.**
To what extent?	The crossing guard was **extremely** cold.

Identifying Adjectives and Adverbs

Identify the boldfaced word as an adjective or an adverb. Write **ADJ** or **ADV** on the line.

1. Snowstorms don't strike **our** city often. _____

2. However, when they do, they **always** shut the town down. _____

3. The weather forecasters were predicting a record snowfall of perhaps **14** inches. _____

4. **Many** residents hurried to the grocery stores to stock up on bread and milk. _____

5. They had heard news about how **this** storm had affected other places. _____

6. The snowplows were **ready** to keep the streets clear and safe. _____

7. The snow fell **gently** at first, falling in big flakes. _____

8. Then the wind picked up, eventually turning into a **screaming** gale. _____

9. Visibility was limited, and snow covered **all** highways. _____

10. Soon many of the roads in and out of town were **completely** closed. _____

11. All residents were urged to stay off the roads until **emergency** workers could clear the highways. _____

12. The wind blew so strongly that utility wires were knocked **down,** and residents were without power. _____

CHAPTER 7

Lesson 1

Using Adjectives and Adverbs

More Practice

A. Identifying Adjectives and the Words They Modify

Underline the adjective once and the word it modifies twice in each of the following sentences. Ignore articles and proper nouns.

1. A large mass of ice and snow that moves slowly is called a glacier.

2. Glaciers are found in polar regions and in mountain passes.

3. Glaciers may measure as much as 10,000 feet in depth.

4. Glaciers develop slowly, as year after year more snow falls in winter than melts in summer.

5. Heavy layers of snow and ice build up, one upon the other.

6. The bottom layer eventually turns into dense crystals of ice.

7. When it is pushed by the weight of all the ice and snow that lie above it, the thick layer of ice starts to move slowly.

8. The pull of gravity on the ice and snow is strong.

9. Ice crystals on the bottom of the glacier alternately melt and freeze.

10. These changes, combined with gravity, make the glacier slide slowly but surely downhill.

B. Identifying Adverbs and the Words They Modify

Underline the word modified by each boldfaced adverb. Then in the blank after each sentence, identify the part of speech of the modified word. Write **V** for a verb, **ADJ** for an adjective, or **ADV** for an adverb.

My doctor's writing is **almost** illegible. *ADJ*

1. The water in this lagoon is almost **always** calm. _____

2. The garbage trucks came down our road **early** this morning. _____

3. The do-it-yourselfer read the directions **very** carefully before beginning the project. _____

4. Sit **down** and tell me all about your trip. _____

5. The sound of the fog horn carried **farther** than we had guessed it would. _____

6. The night watchman was **most** acutely aware of every sound in the building. _____

7. I am **absolutely** certain that this is where I parked my car! _____

8. The surprised hiker peered **curiously** into the cave she had discovered. _____

9. The train stopped **extremely** suddenly when the engineer saw a cow on the tracks. _____

10. As she watched her balloon float **away,** the toddler sobbed uncontrollably. _____

Using Adjectives and Adverbs   *Application*

A. Writing Subjects and Predicates

Complete each of the following sentences by writing an adjective or an adverb in the blank. Then write **ADJ** or **ADV** on the line to identify your word.

1. Skiing is a winter sport that has become extremely _____. _____

2. People love gliding _____ down a snow-covered hill.   _____

3. In the absence of significant snowfall, many ski resorts make
   _____ snow for enthusiasts who can't wait for the real thing. _____

4. Skiers must be _____ and _____.   _____

5. Also, skiers should _____ be aware of snow conditions
   and must adjust their style to the snow.   _____

6. Even though snow may look soft and fluffy, in reality it can
   be _____ hard and unforgiving if you fall.   _____

7. Cross-country skiing offers a _____ alternative to
   downhill skiing.   _____

8. Instead of skiing downhill, cross-country skiers glide
   on _____ terrain.   _____

9. Freestyle skiers perform _____ stunts on skis.   _____

10. Audiences _____ applaud the skill and daring of freestylers. _____

B. Writing with Adjectives and Adverbs

Imagine that you are snowbound in a mountain cabin for a few days. What thoughts might go through your mind? Who would be with you, and how would those people feel and act? On the lines below, describe the events that transpired during your confinement in the small mountain cabin. Use at least six adjectives and six adverbs in your description.

_____

_____

_____

_____

_____

_____

_____

Name _____   Date _____

Making Comparisons   *Teaching*

Use the **comparative** form of a modifier when comparing two persons, places, things, or actions. Use the superlative when comparing three or more.

Degrees of Comparisons

Positive form makes no comparison.	This canyon is <u>deep</u>.
Comparative form compares two or more.	This canyon is <u>deeper</u> than that one.
Superlative form compares three or more.	This canyon is <u>deepest</u> of all.

Most one-syllable and two-syllable words form the comparative by adding *-er* and the superlative by adding *-est (older, oldest)*. To form the comparative or superlative form of most modifiers with three syllables and modifiers that sound awkward with *-er* and *-est*, combine the regular form with the words *more* and *most (more dangerous, most dangerous)*. To make a negative comparison, use *less* and *least (less possible, least possible)*.

Some familiar modifiers have irregular comparative and superlative forms: *good, better, best; bad, worse, worst; well, better, best; many, more, most; much, more, most.*

A. Identifying Comparative and Superlative Modifiers

On the line, label the boldfaced modifier **P** for positive, **C** for comparative, or **S** for superlative.

1. Which is **better,** a day spent at home or a day spent hiking the Grand Canyon? _____

2. To me, the Grand Canyon is the **most fascinating** spot on the face of the earth. _____

3. I'm not sure of its exact depth, but it is by far the **deepest** canyon I have ever seen. _____

4. At sunset, the canyon shines **red** and purple in the fading glow from the sun. _____

5. At sunrise, hikers attack the canyon trails **most enthusiastically.** _____

6. **Many** visitors hike down to the bottom of the canyon. _____

7. However, **more** visitors are content to view the awesome scene from the rim. _____

B. Using Modifiers in Comparisons

Study the boldfaced modifier in each of the following sentences. If the form of the comparison is correct, write **Correct** on the line. If it is incorrect, write the correct form.

1. All of these vacation spots are attractive, but the Grand Canyon
   attracts me **most.**   _____

2. The weather is **worst** today than it has been all week.   _____

3. Of the four pups in the litter, my dog was the **more friendly.** _____

4. Which was the **more lethal** weapon in the entire medieval arsenal? _____

5. The last speaker spoke **more forcefully** than all the others.   _____

Making Comparisons

More Practice

A. Using Comparisons

Underline the correct form of comparison for each sentence.

1. Which is the (wilder, wildest) river, the Colorado or the Mississippi?

2. The Colorado River is far (tamer, tamest) now than it was in 1869 when John Wesley Powell led an expedition down the river.

3. Nobody was (more interested, most interested) in rivers than Powell.

4. Of all the times in his life, he felt (better, best) when he was exploring a river.

5. Even though he had lost an arm, he handled himself (more expertly, most expertly) than most two-armed people.

6. Though Powell and his nine recruits faced the (most dangerous, more dangerous) rapids possible, their leader never wavered.

7. He was (more surely, most surely) dedicated to exploring the Colorado than ever.

8. Some men on the expedition were (less committed, least committed) than Powell.

9. One man decided that almost any fate was (better, best) than facing another set of rapids, and he left the expedition after one month.

10. Two months later, three more men tried to convince Powell to abandon what they called a suicidal project, but he only became (more determined, most determined) than before.

11. It must have been the (finer, finest) feeling ever for Powell when he and his four remaining companions landed safely at the mouth of the river.

B. Using Modifiers in Comparisons

After each sentence, write the comparative or superlative form of the word in parentheses, choosing the form that is appropriate for that sentence.

1. Which was (funny), the book or the movie?   _____

2. Of all the students in the class, who participates in discussions (much)?   _____

3. Did Dan or Eliot jump (far) in the long jump event?   _____

4. What could be (bad) than a worm in a half-eaten apple?   _____

5. What is the (courageous) thing that you have ever done?   _____

6. The restaurateur noticed (few) patrons on Monday than Tuesday.   _____

7. Of all the bikes in the store window, I like the blue one (good).   _____

8. Which has (little) cholesterol, cottage cheese or mozzarella cheese?   _____

9. Her hair has (many) curls than mine, even after my permanent.   _____

10. After eating the leftover tuna salad, I felt (bad) than before.   _____

CHAPTER 7

Name _____ Date _____

Making Comparisons

Application

A. Using Comparisons in Sentences

Write sentences comparing the following items by using the comparative or superlative form of the modifier in parentheses.

EXAMPLE one spectator sport to all other spectator sports (popular)
Soccer is the most popular spectator sport in the world.

1. telephone reception using one hand-held phone compared to another phone (bad)

_____

2. one storm compared to all others (devastating)

_____

3. one volunteer compared to another (faithfully)

_____

4. one waitress compared to all others in a busy restaurant (tired)

_____

5. a person's health today compared to his health yesterday (well)

_____

6. one character compared to another (realistically)

_____

B. Using Comparisons in Writing

Imagine that you are seeing a natural wonder such as the Grand Canyon or Niagara Falls for the first time. Choose five of the words in the list below, and use their comparative and/or superlative forms in a paragraph describing your visit.

surprising	suddenly	good	beautiful	ancient
gingerly	exhausting	powerful	bad	much
dangerous	carefully	brightly	bravely	memorable

_____

_____

_____

_____

_____

_____

_____

Problems with Comparisons

Teaching

Double Comparisons Do not use both *-er* and *more* to form the comparative. Do not use both *-est* and *most* to form the superlative.

Nonstandard	The prices at this store are more higher than the prices there.
Standard	The prices at this store are higher than the prices there.

Illogical Comparisons Use the word other or else to compare an individual with the rest of its group.

Nonstandard	This store has a better selection than any store.
Standard	This store has a better selection than any other store.

Incomplete Comparisons When you make a compound comparison, use than or as after the first modifier to avoid an incomplete comparison.

Nonstandard	Experienced shoppers are more likely to know a good price.
Standard	Experienced shoppers are more likely to know a good price than novice shoppers would be.

State both parts of a comparison fully if you suspect readers are likely to misunderstand your sentence.

Nonstandard	The money you save by shopping wisely may be more than a new sweater every month.
Standard	The money you save by shopping wisely may be more than the price of a new sweater every month.

A. Using Comparisons Correctly

Choose and underline the correct modifier in each sentence.

1. I have a (higher, more higher) opinion of our senator since he changed his stance on gun control.

2. That is the (most disgustingest, most disgusting) joke I ever heard.

3. The prima ballerina is the (most graceful, most gracefulest) dancer in the troupe.

4. When you are in second place, you try (harder, more harder), they say.

5. Who do you think is (more fitter, fitter), a basketball player or a baseball player?

6. The pollen count today is the (worst, most worst) it's ever been this year.

B. Using Comparisons Logically

In each pair of sentences, choose the sentence that uses modifiers logically and clearly. Underline that sentence.

1. a. You are more likely to get a good seat at the mall theater.

   b. You are more likely to get a good seat at the mall theater than you are at the tiny local theater.

2. a. This restaurant has better burgers than any other restaurant.

   b. This restaurant has better burgers than any restaurant.

3. a. I'd rather spend time at a mall than anywhere.

   b. I'd rather spend time at a mall than anywhere else.

CHAPTER 7

Lesson 3 Problems with Comparisons

More Practice

A. Using Comparisons Correctly

Choose and underline the correct modifier in each sentence.

1. Be sure to use the (sharpest, most sharpest) knife to cut the vegetables.

2. If you like your tea (hotter, more hotter), put it in the microwave for a
few seconds.

3. Plants will grow (more faster, faster) with plenty of water and sunshine.

4. The taste of garlic is even (more stronger, stronger) than that of the onion.

5. The mayor lives in the (oldest, most oldest) house in the city.

B. Correcting Double Comparisons and Illogical and Incomplete Comparisons

Rewrite each sentence to make the comparisons clear and correct.

1. The prices at the discount store are more cheaper.

_____

2. The displays at this mall are more inventive than those at any mall.

_____

3. Of the three malls, the Valleyview Mall is most popularest.

_____

4. The selection at this boutique is more varied than anywhere.

_____

5. Holiday shoppers are less particular.

_____

6. Tracy goes to the mall with her sister more frequently than Lisa.

_____

7. Valleyview Mall rates as high, if not higher, than neighboring malls in customer
satisfaction polls.

_____

_____

8. The fountain in the center of the mall is the most busiest place in the building.

_____

9. The shoe store has sales even more regularly.

_____

10. In the future, will people do their shopping on-line more oftener?

_____

CHAPTER 7

Problems with Comparisons

Application

Lesson 3

A. Proofreading for Comparison Errors

The following paragraph contains several errors involving comparisons. Rewrite each sentence that uses double comparisons, illogical comparisons, or incomplete comparisons on the corresponding line below. If the sentence has no comparison errors, write **Correct** on the line.

      (1) How would you feel if just about everyone you knew thought you had made the most ridiculousest purchase ever? **(2)** That's the situation Secretary of State William Seward found himself in after he purchased Alaska in 1867. **(3)** Not only was Alaska far away, critics said, it was also more useless than any land region in the world. **(4)** They complained that two cents per acre was a higher price, especially for what they called "Seward's Icebox." **(5)** Time, however, has proved critics wrong. **(6)** The purchase that had been ridiculed more than any purchase has paid for itself hundreds of times over. **(7)** With its oil, timber, and minerals, Alaska may have become more valuable than any state. **(8)** Perhaps Seward's Icebox should more appropriately be renamed Seward's Buy of a Lifetime.

1. _____

2. _____

3. _____

4. _____

5. _____

6. _____

7. _____

8. _____

B. Using Comparisons in Writing

Imagine that you are describing your used car to a potential buyer. As you talk about the car, you use at least three comparative and three superlative modifiers, either adjectives or adverbs. Write your sales pitch on the lines below. Use a separate piece of paper, if necessary.

_____

_____

_____

_____

_____

Lesson 4

Other Modifier Problems

Teaching

Avoid these common modifier errors.

This, that, these, and *those* are demonstrative pronouns used as adjectives. They must agree in number with the words they modify (Nonstandard: *these* kind of trees). *Here* and *there* are never used with demonstrative adjectives (Nonstandard: *this here* leaf). *Them* is never used as an adjective in place of *these* or *those* (Nonstandard: *them* branches).

Two pairs of words, *good* and *well, bad* and *badly,* can cause special problems. Study these models of correct uses.

good (adjective and predicate adjective—describes a condition)
Any day I spend outside is a <u>good</u> day.   I feel <u>good</u> when I am outdoors.

well (adverb and predicate adjective—means "healthy")
Poplar trees grow <u>well</u> here.

bad (adjective and predicate adjective—describes a condition)
Keri took a <u>bad</u> fall on a hike.   Who can feel <u>bad</u> on vacation?

A **misplaced modifier** is a word or phrase placed so far away from the word it modifies that the meaning of the sentence is unclear or incorrect.

Misleading	Peter appreciated the mountain scenery <u>walking slowly</u>.
Clearer	<u>Walking slowly</u>, Peter appreciated the mountain scenery.

A **dangling modifier** is a word or phrase that does not clearly modify any noun or pronoun in a sentence.

Misleading	<u>Falling from a high cliff</u>, Peter saw a clear mountain stream.
Clearer	Peter saw a clear mountain stream <u>falling from a high cliff</u>.

Avoid using **double negatives**—two or more negative words used in a sentence to express a single negation. (Nonstandard: *He didn't have no time.*) The words *hardly, barely,* and *scarcely* are considered negative words.

Using the Correct Modifier

In each pair of sentences, underline the sentence that uses modifiers logically and clearly.

1. a. Ever since I had it repaired, the derailleur on my bike has worked well.

   b. Ever since I had it repaired, the derailleur on my bike has worked good.

2. a. The stranger tried to comfort the lost toddler crying loudly.

   b. Crying loudly, the stranger tried to comfort the lost toddler.

3. a. Denice is nervous about playing before those judges at the competition.

   b. Denice is nervous about playing before them judges at the competition.

4. a. Driving down a dark road on a foggy night, the pothole was almost invisible to me.

   b. Driving down a dark road on a foggy night, I could hardly see the pothole.

5. a. Returning after a long illness, Greg couldn't hardly remember his locker combination.

   b. Returning after a long illness, Greg could hardly remember his locker combination.

Other Modifier Problems

More Practice

A. Using the Correct Modifier

Underline the correct word in parentheses in each sentence.

1. Mother took his temperature; he is still not (good, well).

2. (That, That there) vase is almost 200 years old, so be careful with it.

3. (This, These) kind of apple tastes very tart.

4. I just glanced at my test scores; unfortunately, they look (bad, badly).

5. Where are (them, those) stamps I bought at the post office yesterday?

6. Yvette (had, hadn't) scarcely fallen asleep when the phone rang.

7. (That, Those) type of horror movie always unsettles me.

8. I hardly got (no, any) sleep last night because I was so nervous.

9. Don't feel (bad, badly) because you forgot my birthday was today.

10. (This, These) types of errors are symptomatic of a distressing lack of understanding of the concept.

B. Using Modifiers Correctly

Rewrite each sentence to make it clearer and less confusing.

1. Learning how to ski, my instructor gave me special attention.

_____

2. Lasting over four years, over eight million soldiers' lives were claimed by World War I.

_____

_____

3. The umpire ruled that the ball had been fair making a split-second decision.

_____

4. Shaken out of their beds this morning, a serious earthquake surprised the residents of San Francisco.

_____

_____

5. The surgeon explained the procedure to his elderly patient talking slowly and loudly.

_____

_____

6. Frying in the griddle I awoke to the delicious smell of bacon.

_____

CHAPTER 7

Name _____ Date _____

Other Modifier Problems

Application

A. Using Adjectives and Adverbs Correctly

Write sentences in which you use correctly the adjectives and adverbs given.

1. good (predicate adjective) _____

2. well (adverb) _____

3. well (predicate adjective) _____

4. bad (adjective) _____

5. bad (predicate adjective) _____

6. badly (adverb) _____

B. Writing with Adjectives and Adverbs

The following paragraph has several errors involving modifiers. Read each sentence and decide if it has an error. If it does, rewrite it correctly on the corresponding line below. If it is correct, write **Correct** on the corresponding line.

    (1) A recent decision to thin the deer herd in these here city parks has animal lovers up in arms. **(2)** Those who want to protect the deer maintain that the problem is not as severe as officials claim. **(3)** However, I can attest to the fact that there are too many deer speaking from experience. **(4)** I have seen those deer eating my flowers and vegetables. **(5)** Suffering the same kind of damage to their gardens, deer have eaten my neighbors' plantings, too. **(6)** These kind of problems suggest that the deer are breeding too quickly and are running out of adequate forage. **(7)** In other words, the competition to eat is so intense that the deer can't scarcely find enough to eat in the wild. **(8)** Hoping to prevent overcrowding and starvation, the deer herd should, in my opinion, be thinned.

1. _____

2. _____

3. _____

4. _____

5. _____

6. _____

7. _____

8. _____

 **Names**   *Teaching*

Follow these rules of capitalization:

- Capitalize proper nouns and proper adjectives used alone and in compound words. *Examples:* Africa, African, African-American

  Do not capitalize prefixes such as *pre-, anti-,* and *sub-* when they are joined with proper nouns and adjectives. *Example:* anti-Communist

- Capitalize the names and initials of persons. *Example:* Ulysses S. Grant
- Capitalize the abbreviations *Jr.* and *Sr.,* which fall after a person's name.
- Capitalize titles and the abbreviations of titles used with personal names and in direct address. *Example:* Prof. Lopez; Can we interview you, Governor?

  Do not capitalize a title when it follows a person's name or when it is used alone. *Example:* Kathryn Miller was mayor of Grandview.

  Capitalize the following titles when they are used alone to refer to the current holders of the positions: the President, the Vice-President, the Queen, the Pope.

  Do not capitalize the prefix *ex-,* the suffix *-elect,* or the words *former* or *late* when used with a title. *Example:* ex-Mayor Lopez

- Capitalize family names used before a proper noun or used in place of the name. *Example:* Uncle Jerry

  Do not capitalize family names preceded by articles or possessive words. *Example:* my cousin

Capitalizing Names

Underline the letters that should be capitalized in each of the following sentences. If the sentence is already correct, write **Correct** on the line.

1. One of the earliest american writers was the poet anne bradstreet, whose verses bore the stamp of her puritan philosophy.   _____

2. She was the daughter of governor thomas dudley of Massachusetts.   _____

3. Writer Washington Irving wrote about a most unusual character who slept for years—Rip Van Winkle.   _____

4. We studied the works of many American writers with professor mary b. fisher, ph.d.   _____

5. One of her favorite writers was ralph w. emerson, the New England essayist. _____

6. The professor asked the class to read letters written by president thomas jefferson, some to his daughter martha, whom he called patsy.   _____

7. Poet henry w. longfellow tried to warn his countrymen about the horrors of war in his poem "The Arsenal at Springfield."   _____

8. Recently, aunt janet, one of the professor's ex-students, said she enjoys the works of an american-born poet, t.s. eliot, who acquired british citizenship as an adult.   _____

Name _____ Date _____

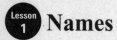
Names

More Practice

A. Capitalizing Names

Underline the letters that should be capitals in each of the following sentences.
If the sentence is already correct, write **Correct** on the line.

1. When I hurt my knee, dr. iswolsky prescribed an anti-inflammatory drug. _____

2. Because johannes brahms was pro-german, he based the text of his
Requiem on excerpts from the german Bible rather than the latin Mass. _____

3. When are you due to address the committee, senator?

4. Writer kurt vonnegut, jr., suggests in his writing that humans should
admit to their own foolishness and destructiveness. _____

5. I bought several yards of scottish wool for my grandmother. _____

6. The city council made the ex-governor an honorary Bostonian. _____

7. I plan to tour the museum with grandma switzer and cousin charlie. _____

8. Talk to one of the english professors about the syllabus for that course. _____

9. "When do you want me to pick you up, Mother?" asked Keri. _____

10. My father, uncle Jim, and dr. gill visited the site of king tut's tomb in Egypt. _____

11. Because he was raised in a greek-american community, the writer harry
mark petrakis can interpret this ethnic immigrant group's experience
in America. _____

12. I know Mrs. Stallings regretted losing her fine Austrian china. _____

B. Capitalizing Correctly

Underline each lowercase letter that should be capitalized in the following paragraph.

(1) Alfred Lord Tennyson was an english poet who lived in the 19th

century. (2) He grew up in Lincolnshire, England, where he was educated by

his father, dr. george clayton tennyson. (3) Alfred Tennyson became interested

in poetry as a child and published some of his early works with his brother

Charles. (4) During college, tennyson joined a spanish revolutionary army.

(5) Although he published poems on a variety of subjects, much of his work

was based on arthurian legend. (6) After publishing many successful

poems, tennyson was named poet laureate of Britain, succeeding william

wordsworth. (7) One of tennyson's most famous poems, "The Charge of the

Light Brigade," was written to celebrate a famous british cavalry unit. (8) Near

the end of his life he gained a seat in the House of Lords and was called baron

tennyson.

Lesson 1

Names

Application

A. Proofreading

Proofread the following first draft of a report. Look especially for errors in capitalization. Draw three lines under each letter that should be capitalized. Draw a slash across any letter that is capitalized when it should be lowercase.

EXAMPLE robert frost was an american Poet .

Robert frost was born in San Francisco, California, but moved to

Lawrence, Massachusetts, with his Mother after the death of his Father. He

did not have much success with his poetry until he moved to England, where

he was able to improve his writing with the aid of the established poets,

william butler yeats, and ezra pound. He then published two volumes of

poetry and returned to the United States, where he immediately became a

popular Poet. Frost's work showed a plain and graceful style, easily accessible

to the american public. His fame became more widespread when he accepted

an invitation by president-elect john f. kennedy to read a poem at his

inauguration. Much of frost's poetry, written in blank verse, celebrates the

beauty of New England farm life.

B. Writing with Capital Letters

Write a brief, imaginary television news "teaser"—a quick preview of stories that will be reported on fully during a later news program. Include at least five names, using the guidelines described in this lesson. Include at least one proper noun, one proper adjective, one name with Jr. or Sr., and the name and title of a government official.

_____

_____

_____

_____

_____

_____

_____

_____

_____

Lesson 2 · Other Names and Places   *Teaching*

Follow these rules of capitalization:

- Capitalize the names of ethnic groups, races, languages, and nationalities, as well as adjectives formed from these names. *Example:* Chinese
- Capitalize all names referring to religions and their followers, sacred days and writings, and deities. *Examples:* Lutheran; Rosh Hashanah; Koran; Aton

  Do not capitalize the words *god* and *goddess* in reference to ancient mythology.
- Capitalize the names of specific places, such as cities or states (Detroit, Michigan), regions (the Midwest), countries (Canada), parts of the world (Europe), land features (the Alps), bodies of water (the Mediterranean Sea), and streets and highways (Main Street, Eisenhower Expressway).

  Do not capitalize words that refer to directions of the compass. *Example:* Drive east for five miles.
- Capitalize the names of historical events (World War II); historical periods (Reconstruction); and calendar items, such as days, months, and holidays (Thanksgiving Day).

Capitalizing Names and Places

Underline the words that should be capitalized in each of the following sentences. If the item is capitalized correctly, write **Correct** on the line.

1. Each year, more than 18 million tourists visit washington, D.C.   _____

2. The district of columbia, another name for the city, is located at the junction of two rivers, the potomac and the anacostia.   _____

3. Both virginia, which is southwest of D.C., and maryland, which is north, east, and southeast of the city, gave up land in order to form the capital city. _____

4. Pierre Charles L'Enfant, a french architect, designed the city in a very orderly way.   _____

5. The numbered streets run north to south and the lettered streets run east to west.   _____

6. The diagonal avenues, such as Massachusetts avenue and pennsylvania avenue, are named after states that played prominent roles in early american history.   _____

7. All presidents but George Washington have lived in the White House, which was burned by the british during the war of 1812.   _____

8. Special tours of the White House gardens are offered in april and october. _____

9. Union Station is a transportation hub that also has a large food court with restaurants boasting chinese, italian, Greek, and japanese cuisine.   _____

10. The many famous churches in the city include the National Cathedral, which is episcopalian, and the National Shrine of the Immaculate Conception, which is roman catholic.   _____

11. Washington, D.C., is a great place to be for the fourth of july, when it hosts a grand fireworks display.   _____

CHAPTER 8

Lesson 2 · Other Names and Places

More Practice

A. Capitalizing Names and Places

Underline the words that should be capitalized in each of the following sentences.

1. Humans are always searching for answers to the mysteries of the universe; those who follow islam look to the sacred book, the koran, written in arabic.

2. To christians, the bible is god's word; to hindus, the veda is sacred.

3. The talmud is the authoritative body of jewish tradition.

4. Some peoples in south america, europe, and africa searched the sky for answers.

5. The ancient maya, who lived in mexico, were excellent astonomers.

6. When astronomers in ancient egypt and greece began to study the skies of the northern hemisphere, they divided distinct groups of stars into constellations.

7. Ancient european and african astronomers looked up into the skies over the mediterranean sea and wondered how everything came to be.

8. People from all over the world brought their curiosity about life and the universe with them to north america.

9. The united states began serious space exploration when it launched its first satellite from cape canaveral.

10. From the east coast to the west coast, americans became fascinated by the possibility of space travel and the knowledge it would bring them.

11. Cape canaveral is located in the south, on the east-central coast of florida, ten miles north of cocoa beach.

12. The russians had launched a similar satellite at an earlier date, much to the dismay of americans, who had planned on being the first in space.

13. When President John Kennedy moved to pennsylvania avenue in washington, D.C., he vowed that the united states would have a man on the moon soon.

14. A new era, the space age, promised new ways to answer the ancient questions.

B. Capitalizing Names of Places in a Paragraph

Underline the words that should be capitalized in the following paragraph.

Paris, france, is one of the largest cities in europe. It was first called Lutetia, but when the romans gained control, they renamed it civitas parisiorum. The seine river runs through the city and divides in into the left bank and the right bank. Paris is a relatively flat city, and its highest point, montmartre, is only 423 feet above sea level. The French national holiday is july 14th, bastille day. The champs élysées, a famous parisian street, is known for its multitude of expensive shops and restaurants. One of the best known gothic cathedrals, the catholic Cathedral of Notre Dame, is located on an island in the seine.

Lesson 2 — Other Names and Places

Application

A. Proofreading for Capital Letters

Read the following advertisement for a tour to a vacation spot. Draw three lines under any letters that should be capitalized but are not. Draw a slash across any letter that is capitalized incorrectly.

> **EXAMPLE** Someday I would like to travel to europe and see the great Churches and other historic buildings there.

Euro Travel has just announced a 14-day tour of the benelux nations, including Luxembourg City, bruges, and amsterdam. On monday you start in luxembourg city, where you can enjoy european charm at its best. The city's population is less than 100,000 and almost all residents speak Letzeburgesch (a germanic language), french, german, and usually English. The city boasts an old medieval section situated on a high plateau, the bock peninsula, which overlooks the neighboring alzette valley. The city's 16th-century Grand Ducal Palace is not to be missed. Next, on to bruges, one of the best-preserved Medieval Cities in europe. It features more than 50 bridges arching over its canals. You will enjoy a splendid tour of the belgian city, including its marketplace. Last, you will visit amsterdam, a city in Northeast netherlands, where you will take a boat tour over some of the 50 miles of canals. In addition, you will have a chance to visit the Rijksmuseum in Amsterdam and see its world-famous collections of dutch and flemish paintings.

B. Capitalizing Names of Places

On the lines, write a specific and detailed description of where you live, including your street address, city, county, state, region of the country, country, continent, hemisphere, planet, star system, and galaxy.

_____

_____

_____

_____

_____

_____

_____

Organizations & Other Subjects

Lesson 3

Teaching

Follow these rules of capitalization:

- Capitalize all important words in the names of organizations, including teams and businesses, and including schools, hospitals, and institutions; government bodies, and political parties. *Examples:* Hilldale Chamber of Commerce, Control Corporation, Parkdale Hospital, Congress, Democratic Party

- Capitalize names of stars, planets, galaxies, constellations, and other heavenly bodies. *Examples:* Sirius, Neptune, Milky Way, Orion (but not sun and moon)

  Capitalize earth only when it is used with other capitalized astronomical terms. Do not capitalize *earth* when it is preceded by the article *the.*

- Capitalize names of specific ships, trains, airplanes, and spacecraft. *Example: Half Moon*

- Capitalize names of monuments, memorials, and other landmarks. *Example:* Washington Monument

- Capitalize names of school subjects when they refer to specific courses. Do not capitalize the general names of school subjects, except language courses. *Examples:* Biology 2, French, history

  Capitalize the words *freshman, sophomore, junior,* and *senior* only when they are part of a proper noun. *Example:* Senior Awards Assembly

- Capitalize the names of awards, special events, and brand names. *Examples:* Medal of Honor, Founder's Celebration, Tasty Tidbits

Identifying Correct Capitalization

Underline the words or letters that should be capitals in each of the following sentences.

1. The vietnam veterans memorial attracted more visitors than any other memorial in the city.

2. All of the freshmen are required to go to freshman orientation on the first day of school.

3. The video awards honor the best music videos of the year.

4. The symbol of the democratic party is the donkey, while the republican party's symbol is the elephant.

5. Incoming students must take history, english I, math, and french or spanish.

6. Charles Lindbergh flew the *spirit of st. louis* on the first solo nonstop flight across the Atlantic Ocean.

7. At least one satellite orbits every planet except mercury and venus.

8. Every January the president addresses congress in the state of the union address.

9. Many tourists visit Boston to see fanueil hall, old north church, and fenway park.

10. The north atlantic treaty organization has its headquarters in Brussels.

11. The international red cross aids victims of emergencies all over the earth.

12. On April 14, 1912, the *titanic* struck an iceberg and sank on its maiden voyage.

13. Rings encircle the planets saturn, neptune, and uranus.

14. The world cup, the soccer championship game, holds tournaments for both women's and men's teams.

Lesson 3 **Organizations & Other Subjects**   *More Practice*

A. Capitalizing Names of Organizations and Other Subjects

Underline each letter that should be capitalized in the following sentences.

1. An interesting field trip supplemented american architecture I for us.

2. The freshman class visited a home built before the american revolution.

3. I photographed George Washington's Mount Vernon with my greatshot camera.

4. In 1853 the mount vernon ladies' association purchased Mount Vernon and repaired it.

5. That same spring day we also visited Monticello, the home of Thomas Jefferson, a leader in the democratic-republican party.

6. We heard about events during his administration, for example, the maiden voyage of Robert Fulton's steamship, the *clermont.*

7. Later we visited the university of virginia, founded by Jefferson.

8. Our guide was a senior and a member of the daughters of the american revolution.

9. She told us about Jefferson's many accomplishments, some of which were so notable that he would have been worthy of the nobel prize.

B. Capitalizing Correctly

Underline the words in each sentence that should be capitalized. Then write them correctly on the corresponding lines below. If a sentence is capitalized correctly, write **Correct.**

(1) Starting this fall, all freshman and sophomores can now enroll in astronomy 101, one of the winners of the annual students' choice award. **(2)** The course will begin by looking at the circumstances surrounding the founding of the National aeronautics and Space administration in 1958. **(3)** Since nasa and much of its funding rely on the consent of congress, we will examine this relationship and its impact on the space program. **(4)** We will study in detail the beginnings of space exploration, starting with the launch of *sputnik I* in 1957 by the Soviet Union. **(5)** We will then examine the space race that culminated in the United States landing *apollo 11* on the moon in 1969. **(6)** We'll look at recent efforts such as the unmanned spacecraft *galileo,* which sent back photographs and information when it orbited earth, venus, and jupiter. **(7)** The course will end with student presentations about the Russian space station *mir* and the international space station. **(8)** Selected students will have the honor of presenting their work at the Astronomy Department's forum called space exploration in the future. **(9)** This course is a prerequisite for all further classes in astronomy.

1. _____   6. _____

2. _____   7. _____

3. _____   8. _____

4. _____   9. _____

5. _____

Lesson 3 Organizations & Other Subjects — *Application*

A. Proofreading for Capitalization Errors

Read the following speech given at a university awards ceremony. Draw three lines under any letters that should be capitalized but are not. Draw a slash across any letter that is capitalized in error.

EXAMPLE Our Ørganization welcomes you all to the brooks auditorium today.

The board of citizens in space is pleased to announce the recipient of the great leap in space award—Dr. Annamaria Sandal. Dr. Sandal, who holds a Ph.D. from stanford university, is currently the president of venus international corporation. Prior to her work at VIC, she worked for the department of state. The Scientific Programs run by Dr. Sandal have done much to advance the cause of safe space exploration for ordinary citizens. In fact, VIC has collaborated with us on our Mission to one day see a civilian on the moon, or even mars. Dr. Sandal also teaches a course to Senior Astronomy and Physics majors at massachusetts institute of technology. We are pleased to present this award, modeled after the Space Shuttle *atlantis,* to the worthy Dr. Annamaria Sandal.

B. Using Capitalization in Writing

Try to imagine your future—the college or university you might attend and the courses you might take there. Then imagine the organization or business you might work for and the political party to which you might belong and why. Consider the places you might visit and the landmarks you want to see someday. Finally, think of any awards you could earn in your lifetime. Write a paragraph in which you describe your possible future. Be sure to use capital letters correctly in your paragraph. Include the following names:

a college or university   a landmark or a monument
a business or institution   an award
a political party

_____

_____

_____

_____

_____

_____

_____

Name _____ Date _____

First Words and Titles

Teaching

Follow these rules of capitalization:

- Capitalize the first words of sentences and of lines of traditional poetry.
- Capitalize the first word of a direct quotation, if it is a complete sentence. Do not capitalize a direct quotation if it is a sentence fragment.
- Capitalize the first word of each item in an outline and the letters that introduce major subsections.
- Capitalize the pronoun *I*.
- Capitalize the first, last, and all other important words in titles, including verbs; but not conjunctions, articles, or prepositions with fewer than five letters.

Capitalizing First Words and Titles

Underline the words that should be capitalized in each of the following items. If the item is capitalized correctly, write **Correct** on the line.

1. my favorite Shakespeare comedy is *the taming of the shrew*. _____

2. "your statement about me was inaccurate," fumed the candidate, "so i demand a retraction." _____

3. Tim replied, "the photograph was taken at dusk." _____

4. i decided to outline my speech on El Salvador in this way: _____
   I. historical introduction from colonization through present
   II. the people
      a. population and ancestry
      b. housing

5. i like the line from Whittier's "snowbound": "so all night long the storm roared on." _____

6. in 1939 Moss Hart and George F. Kaufman wrote the witty comedy *the man who came to dinner*. _____

7. listen, my children, and you shall hear
   of the midnight ride of Paul Revere,
   Henry W. Longfellow, "Paul Revere's Ride" _____

8. have you ever read James Michener's *tales of the south pacific?* _____

9. the principal announced, "the assembly will be held in the new auditorium." _____

10. "at this time of year," the meteorologist explained, "we lose about three minutes of daylight every day." _____

11. the congressman referred to today's incident as "an issue of the utmost importance for national security." _____

12. "it's such a beautiful day," said Andy. "let's go for a walk." _____

Lesson 4

First Words and Titles

More Practice

A. Capitalizing First Words and Titles

In the following sentences, underline the words that should be capitalized but are not. If the sentence contains no capitalization errors, write **Correct** on the line.

1. When i get older, i want to become a veterinarian. _____

2. this summer the assigned reading is *the age of innocence,* by
   Edith Wharton. _____

3. The film critic said the new movie was "a suspenseful thriller." _____

4. while i nodded, nearly napping, suddenly there came a tapping,
   as of some one gently rapping, rapping at my chamber door.
   Edgar Allan Poe, "The Raven" _____

5. Abigail asked, "are there any sharks at this aquarium?" _____

6. One of the most popular books ever written is *great expectations.* _____

7. "admittedly, the future holds potential dangers," said the candidate,
   "but it also holds great promise." _____

8. our team was losing the game until i hit the home run. _____

9. "The vacation," Malik said, "was the best i ever had." _____

10. I celebrate myself, and sing myself,
    and what I assume you shall assume,
    for every atom belonging to me as good belongs to you.
    Walt Whitman, "Song of Myself" _____

11. Almost everyone knows of the play *our town.* _____

12. last night, Gavin and i rented a video. _____

B. Capitalizing First Words in Outlines

Underline each letter that should be capitalized in the following outline.
Ukraine
  I. location
 II. climate facts
      a. average temperature in summer
      b. average temperature in winter
      c. average annual precipitation
III. the people

Lesson 4

First Words and Titles

Application

A. Writing a Conversation

Continue this conversation by two people leaving a theater after a play. Include at least four titles, as the speakers compare this play and its actors to other plays or movies they have seen. Be sure to capitalize the quotations and titles correctly.

"I can see why the critics praised this movie. The review I read compared it to *Macbeth,* but updated," said Beth.

"I thought the film was okay, but I've seen better," replied Martin.

_____

_____

_____

_____

_____

B. Writing an Outline Using Capital Letters Correctly

Read the following brief report. Then write a short outline for it on the lines below. Be sure to capitalize correctly.

     Harry Truman had an active life before entering the realm of politics. Truman grew up in Independence, Missouri, where he was an avid reader and piano player. He was a farmer until the outbreak of World War I, during which he became a 2nd Lieutenant. After the war, he opened a men's clothing store and became involved in a few other unsuccessful business ventures.

     For two years Truman was a Jackson County judge and then held two four-year terms as the presiding county judge. Afterwards, he won a seat in the United States Senate, where he led a committee to end waste and fraud in the defense programs. In 1944 he was nominated as Franklin Delano Roosevelt's vice-president and succeeded to the presidency himself upon Roosevelt's death in 1945.

The Life of Harry Truman

_____

_____

_____

_____

_____

_____

_____

_____

Abbreviations

Lesson 5

Teaching

Follow these rules of capitalization for abbreviation:

- Capitalize abbreviations of the names of cities, states, countries, and other places. *Examples:* L.A. (Los Angeles); TX (Texas), UAE (United Arab Emirates) (Do not use a state abbreviation in formal writing—use only in an address or reference).
- Capitalize abbreviations related to time. *Examples:* B.C., A.D., A.M., P.M.
- Capitalize abbreviations of organizations and agencies. (These abbreviations usually do not take periods.) *Examples:* NCAA (National Collegiate Athletic Association)

Capitalizing Abbreviations

Underline the letters that should be capitalized in each of the following sentences. If the sentence is already correct, write **Correct** after the sentence.

1. Tonight at 6 P.M., the New York City news will have special coverage of the nyc elections.

2. The new series on ancient Egypt begins with a study of the Pyramid of Khafre, built around 2530 b.c.

3. The season finale of my favorite comedy begins at 9 P.M.

4. The financial coverage on the news network uscn will feature an analysis of the euro in the EU (European Union).

5. Between 7 a.m. and 9 a.m., the news channel displays the weather forecast every 20 minutes.

6. The new president of the naacp is a guest on a talk show tonight.

7. My soccer coach actually played in a soccer game between the UK and France.

8. The traditional abbreviation for Florida is *Fla.*, but the postal abbreviation is fl.

9. The match sponsored by the Clearview Wrestling Association (cwa) should be over by 11 P.M.

10. The reporter is standing in the Roman Colosseum, built in a.d. 80.

11. Her address is 123 Maple St., Boston, ma, 02116.

12. In preparation for the tax season, a representative from the irs will appear on the morning talk show to answer questions.

Lesson 5 **Abbreviations** *More Practice*

A. Capitalizing Abbreviations

Underline the letters that should be capitals in each of the following sentences.
If the sentence is already correct, write **Correct** on the line beside it.

1. If I send this letter to Grand Canyon, az, will it get to the national park there? _____

2. The Environmental Protection Agency is more commonly referred to as the epa. _____

3. Charlemagne became emperor of the Romans in a.d. 800. _____

4. Hawaii, the last state to be admitted to the United States, uses hi as its
postal code. _____

5. The cia is part of a larger intelligence community in the United States. _____

6. The Zhou dynasty ruled China from the 11th to the 3rd century b.c. _____

7. The only part of the address I remember is Boise, ID. _____

8. All 35 nations in the Western Hemisphere, but one, are members of the oas,
the Organization of American States. _____

9. Octavian, later known as Augustus, was emperor of the Roman empire from
29 b.c. to a.d. 14. _____

10. If it is 2:00 p.m. on the East Coast, it is 11:00 a.m. on the West Coast. _____

11. Betty Friedan was the first president of NOW, the National Organization
for Women, which was founded in 1966. _____

B. Capitalizing Correctly

Underline each lowercase letter that should be capitalized in the following paragraph.

(1) This week marks the start of two new compelling television series.

(2) On Tuesday at 8:00 p.m., the new series on great moments in sports will

debut. **(3)** Each week, the show will highlight different sports arenas, starting

with stadiums in nyc. **(4)** A new series about women in power premieres on

Thursday at 9:00 p.m. and will be repeated Friday at 11:30 a.m. **(5)** The first

show features Cleopatra, the last ruler in the Ptolemaic dynasty, who ruled till

30 b.c. **(6)** The dynasty was founded in 323 b.c. by Ptolemy, one of Alexander

the Great's generals. **(7)** The next episode will feature Catherine the Great of

Russia, who ruled Russia from a.d. 1762 to 1796.

Lesson 5 **Abbreviations**   *Application*

A. Proofreading

The following paragraph is a draft of a news report for a television news anchor. Not all of the abbreviations have been written correctly, making it difficult for the anchor to read the report smoothly. Proofread the report, looking especially for errors in the capitalization of abbreviations. Draw three lines under each letter that should be capitalized.

> **EXAMPLE** A meeting beginning at 9:00 a.m. tomorrow is of interest to people around the world.

This week the North Atlantic Treaty Organization is having a summit in Washington, d.c. Leaders from the member nations will be meeting at 9:00 a.m. tomorrow. The conference is not scheduled to end until 5:30 p.m. on Friday. The heads of state will gather at the White House to have their picture taken following an exclusive interview this afternoon. The Department of State will be host to a special gathering of the foreign ministers. For the new Secretary of State, this will be her first major discussion at the dos. This important nato summit is taking place only a week before the United Nations assembly in New York. The meeting was scheduled so that the heads of state could go directly to the un to discuss the current state of the European Union. The eu held important consultations earlier this month in preparation for the Un speeches. Washington, D.c. and ny will be bustling with political activity in the following weeks.

B. Writing with Capital Letters

Make up the name of a fictional school organization and abbreviate it. Then write the secretary's report for a meeting of that organization. The group has been working on several projects with other organizations in different cities, states, and even countries. The report lists times and places of meetings and functions. Use at least five abbreviations in your report. Use a separate piece of paper, if necessary.

_____

_____

_____

_____

_____

_____

Lesson 1

Periods and Other End Marks

Teaching

Use a **period** after these types of sentences:

Declarative sentence	My birthday is June 3.
Imperative sentence	Blow out the candles.
Indirect question	Andy asked what my favorite kind of cake is.

Use an **exclamation point** after these groups of words:

Exclamatory sentence	What a beautiful morning it is!
Strong interjection	Surprise!
Words that express a sound	Bang!

Use a **question mark** after these types of sentences:

Interrogative sentence	How old are you?
Declarative sentence that asks a question	You celebrated yesterday?

Use a period with abbreviations and initials *(Examples:* St., Sr., hr., min., ft., in.) and after each number or letter in an outline or list.

Do **not** use periods with metric measurements *(Examples:* cm, kg), acronyms *(Examples:* NASA, SEATO), abbreviations that are pronounced letter by letter *(Example:* NCAA), state names in postal addresses *(Examples:* TX, NE), or points on a compass (N, S, E, W).

Using Periods and Other End Marks

Add end marks after each sentence and periods after abbreviations as necessary in the following items.

1. What a party that was for Chuck's birthday
2. Do you think I'm exaggerating when I say that his stack of invitations was at least five inches high
3. Even Mr Johnston, Sr, received one
4. The party began at 7:00 PM, didn't it
5. All of the birthday invitations included an RSVP
6. The invitation ot Leo White, Jr, with the address 545 Wilberforce Dr, South Bend, IN was returned
7. His parents debated whether to hold the party at the Jones Bros Party Center or at their E Main Ave home
8. Chuck's favorite gift was an official college football
9. I gave him an 8-oz bottle of cologne
10. Be sure to film Chuck opening that huge gift
11. There was plenty of pizza from T J Rossi's Italian Restaurant on Adams Blvd
12. What an enormous cake we had (one yd by two ft)
13. I   Party decorations

     A Red and white streamers

     B One hundred eighty balloons

Lesson 1 — Periods and Other End Marks   *More Practice*

A. Using End Marks

Add periods, question marks, and exclamation points where they are needed in the following sentences.

1. Is the IRS office open after 5:00 PM on Friday
2. Help I can't turn off the water
3. Dr Williams and Dr Thomas are both excellent surgeons
4. I mailed the letter to 29 Randolph St, Meadville, PA 16335
5. Kim asked if she could come with us
6. The ambulance sped down Grove Dr and turned onto Highland Ave in moments
7. Have you ever seen a live squid I have
8. Does Prof Winters have a class scheduled in Rm 222
9. Lyndon B Johnson initiated the War on Poverty
10. Faith poured 3 ml of water into the beaker
11. Wait Don't leave before I finish my homework for US history
12. Good heavens How did that dog get in here
13. What a ridiculous story
14. UNICEF and UNESCO are both agencies of the United Nations
15. Report to the principal's office on your way out
16. Did I understand correctly You think I forgot your birthday Impossible
17. Does the sign on the door of the detective agency say "Lost and Found Corp"
18. Your shopping list is short, with only two items:

    1 milk
    2 bread

B. Using Periods in Outlines

Add periods where they are needed in the following outline.

Birthdays of Famous Americans

I October

  A Oct 1 to Oct 7

    1 William Boeing, founder of an airplane company, Oct 1, 1888

    2 Jimmy Carter, 39th President of the US, Oct 1, 1924

  B Oct 8 to Oct 15

    1 Eleanor Roosevelt, First Lady and UN delegate, Oct 11, 1884

    2 Dwight D Eisenhower, 34th President of the US, Oct 14, 1918

II November

  A Nov 1 to Nov 8

    1 Daniel Boone, explorer, Nov 2, 1724

    2 John P Sousa, bandleader and composer, Nov 6, 1854

Lesson 1

Periods and Other End Marks

Application

A. Proofreading

Below is a first draft by a columnist writing quickly just to get her ideas down on paper. Occasionally, she neglected to use periods and end marks correctly. Read her first draft below and add periods, question marks, and exclamation points where necessary. To insert a question mark or exclamation point, insert a caret and write in the needed punctuation mark above the caret. To insert a period, use this symbol ⊙ at the appropriate place.

The fourth month of the year is filled with the birthdays of famous

Americans Did you know that four presidents were born in April Two of them

were from Virginia: Thomas Jefferson, born on Apr 13 in Albemarle County,

and James Monroe, born Apr 28 in Monrovia James Buchanan, the 15th

president, and Ulysses S Grant, the 18th president, were also April babies

Nineteenth-century naturalist, John Burroughs, and ornithologist and painter,

John James Audubon, claim this month as well (What detailed paintings of

birds Audubon drew) Were other famous Americans born in April, or in your

birthday month Check in any encyclopedia under the name of your birth

month A few surprises await you

B. Using End Marks in an Outline

If you were planning a party, what decisions and plans would you have to make? Which decisions should be made weeks or days before the party, and which issues must be attended to just before the guests arrive? On the form below, outline your plans for a party you could give someday—either to celebrate a holiday or a special event in someone's life. Give the outline a title, and identify two major divisions, for example, long-range planning and short-range details. Then suggest three main ideas under each division. Be sure to punctuate correctly.

Title:

I _____

   A _____

   B _____

   C _____

II _____

   A _____

   B _____

   C _____

Lesson 2

Commas in Sentence Parts

Teaching

Use commas after introductory words or mild interjections such as *oh, yes, no,* and *well;* after an introductory prepositional phrase that contains additional prepositional phrases; after verbal phrases, adverb clauses, and adverbs used as introductory elements; and after an introductory infinitive or participial phrase.

> **Well,** I have never ridden in a sailboat.
> **In a little boat on the ocean,** you can get away from daily stresses.
> **Usually,** that pleasure is out of my reach.
> **To understand the joy of sailing,** you must try it yourself.
> **Feeling adventurous,** I decided to try the sport.

Use commas to set off words of direct address, such as names and titles. Use commas to set off parenthetical expressions—words that interrupt the flow of thought in a sentence such as these: *however, therefore, for example, I suppose, moreover*—and to separate a question tagged onto the end of a sentence.

> **By the way, David,** you have sailed before, **haven't you?**

Use commas to set off nonessential clauses and participial phrases, and nonessential appositives and appositive phrases.

> The instructor, **who is also a friend of mine,** showed me his boat, *Fancy- Free.*

Use a comma before a conjunction joining two independent clauses of a compound sentence.

> He was an experienced sailor, **but** this was my first time on a sailboat.

Use a comma after every item in a series of three or more except the last one. Use a comma between two or more adjectives of equal rank that modify the same noun.

> On a **cool, windy** day we sailed past other **boats, the docks, and the lighthouse.**

Using Commas Correctly

Insert commas where necessary in the following sentences.

1. We sailed past two ore freighters a speedboat and several water-skiers when we ventured outside the harbor.

2. Our craft glided by the lighthouse which has guided ships into the harbor for years.

3. Yes skill is needed to sail a sloop on a windy day.

4. To monitor the weather most sailors carry a shortwave radio on board their boats.

5. Tipping over dangerously close to the water our sailboat became unstable until Paul shifted his weight and slacked off on the mainsail.

6. You did remember to pack the extra life jackets didn't you?

7. You can move the mainsail to catch the breeze or I will start the engine to take us back to port.

8. In the well-stocked galley on our little boat I can prepare simple or elaborate meals while you sail.

9. The spinnaker sail is usually made of strong elastic nylon.

CHAPTER 9

Lesson 2 Commas in Sentence Parts

More Practice

A. Using Commas

Insert commas where they are needed in each sentence. If no commas are necessary, write **None** on the line.

1. Please buy bread lettuce milk and orange juice at the grocery store. _____

2. The abandoned rustic barn is no longer sound enough to use. _____

3. Do you know Brian why the North Pole has such a cold climate? _____

4. Yes it is because the sun never rises far above the horizon there. _____

5. Naturally the bus left early on the only day I was running late. _____

6. Kurt likes to ski because it is good exercise because he likes to be outdoors and because he enjoys moving quickly. _____

7. After school we stopped at the library. _____

8. The security guard who stands inside the bank was a high school athlete. _____

9. To stay under budget our class decided against an expensive band for the prom. _____

10. Marissa is a conscientious helpful assistant. _____

11. The United Nations, which meets in New York City, is now in session. _____

12. Before the children's parents left they gave Chandra the telephone number where they could be reached. _____

13. This excellent movie I suppose will be nominated for an award. _____

14. Lisa looked up the number and made the call. _____

15. The cat having been left alone all weekend complained loudly when its owners returned. _____

B. Using Commas in Writing

Insert commas where they are needed in the following paragraphs.

Hunting whales seems unthinkable to us doesn't it? Well earlier in the history of our country whaling was an important industry. In the 1600s the colonists hunted right whales off the Atlantic coast. By the end of the 1700s right whaling had declined and sperm whaling had expanded throughout the Atlantic and into the South Pacific. Sperm whales produced three valuable products: sperm oil a fuel for lamps; spermaceti an ingredient in candles; and ambergris the base for expensive perfumes. Whaling was a profitable respectable business.

The 19th century saw a change in whaling. Lured by the dream of striking it rich in the California goldfields young men who had formerly signed up for whaling crews headed west. During the Civil War many whaling ships were sunk by the Confederate forces. Finally with the rise of the U.S. petroleum industry in the late 1800s whaling declined even further. Today, Americans no longer hunt whales but instead work to protect them.

Commas in Sentence Parts

Lesson 2

Application

A. Writing with Commas

Add commas where they are needed in the following paragraph.

The sleek beautiful clipper ship is perhaps the best-known sailing ship built in the 1800s. Prized for its speed the clipper ship had a slender hull and up to six rows of sails on each mast. Its name was a derivation of *clip,* meaning "to move swiftly." Indeed it could move at a top speed of 20 knots. Clipper ships carried tea from China wool from Australia and passengers and supplies to the goldfields in California. From New York on the East Coast the clipper ships could sail around the tip of South America and dock at San Francisco in about 100 days. The greatest designer of these ships was Donald McKay a Canadian. At his shipyard in East Boston, Massachusetts McKay constructed over 30 ships. One of them *Great Republic* was the largest such boat ever built. Sailing on such a ship would be quite an adventure don't you think?

B. Using Commas in Writing

Rewrite the sentences by following the directions in parentheses.

1. The crew leader picked up a large toolbox. (Include a series of items.)

_____

_____

2. Together, the crew members were going to repair the house. (Include two adjectives of equal rank that modify the same noun.)

_____

3. The crew set to work. (Add an introductory clause.)

_____

4. The crew leader said, "This kind of work is rewarding." (Add a noun of direct address and a question tagged on the end of the sentence.)

_____

_____

5. The owners were grateful for the help with their house. (Include a nonessential clause.)

_____

6. The crew had a late dinner. They planned what they would do tomorrow. (Combine the sentences with a conjunction.)

_____

_____

Lesson 3 Using Commas for Clarity

Teaching

Use a comma to separate words that might be misread.

> The Internet is useful, for researchers can find what they need there.

Use a comma to replace an omitted word or words.

> Some people use the phone to communicate; others, the Internet.

Use a comma with antithetical phrases that make a contrast by using words such as *not* or *unlike*.

> The Internet, unlike magazines, contains up-to-date information.

Use a comma before a coordinating conjunction (*and, but, or*) to avoid a comma splice, an error that occurs when you use a comma to separate two main clauses. Other ways to eliminate a comma splice are to use a period or a semicolon to separate the clauses.

> People who enjoy the Internet can almost become addicted to it, <u>and</u> they sometimes spend most of their day going from one Web site to the next.

Using Commas Correctly

Insert commas where necessary in the following sentences.

1. I use my laptop to access the Internet; my friend his full-sized PC.

2. Marla bought a book over the Internet and it was delivered to her the next day.

3. The first hyperlink not the second takes you to the singer's Web page.

4. Before the Internet information was not as readily available.

5. At home, I use the Internet to look for information about my favorite bands but at school I use it to research my project.

6. Jonathan buys his airline tickets via the Internet; his brother by phone.

7. Before on-line banking bills were always being misplaced at home.

8. Now customers can access their accounts easily and they can pay bills electronically.

9. The on-line course I am taking unlike regular classes lets me read the lecture at any time.

10. I am grateful for the Internet is easy to use with a minimum of training.

11. All it takes is a little experience not an expensive course.

12. This radio station unlike its competitors broadcasts its shows over the Internet.

13. Without the Internet finding articles for my research papers would be more time-consuming.

14. The author's Web site not the publisher's page announces her book signing dates.

15. When we logged on the Internet service provider told me I had new mail.

16. Jonas used to go to the record store every week to buy new CD's but now he shops on-line and he can even listen to the CD's before he buys them.

17. Before I found this search engine finding information about gardening was very difficult.

18. Erik uses the phone book to find phone numbers; Joshua the Internet directories.

Lesson 3 — **Using Commas for Clarity**   *More Practice*

A. Using Commas Correctly

Add commas where necessary in the following sentences.

1. In short steps have been taken to remedy the situation.
2. The whale and the dolphin unlike other ocean animals are mammals.
3. The cats were yowling by the back yard fence and Alicia could not concentrate.
4. President Reagan was a Republican; President Clinton a Democrat.
5. Harry Truman believed that the atomic bomb would end the war; conventional forces prolong it.
6. Jackie Robinson was an outstanding hitter but he was also a great runner and base-stealer.
7. Some people enjoy listening to classical music; others jazz.
8. Although my aunt is a cook at a restaurant, it was my mother not my aunt who won the baking contest.
9. Helen plays the piano; Sarah the violin.
10. Quilts are warm bed covers but many are also fine examples of folk art.
11. This room in contrast to the white walls of the rest of the house is painted blue.
12. To Lola Marie was her best friend and always would be.
13. The tiny mouse not the great lion turned out to be the hero of the story.
14. After coloring my little sister put away her crayons and coloring books.
15. The thunderstorm caused many power outages and some people were without electricity for days.
16. The contestants say eyewitnesses, were coached before the quiz show.

B. Using the Comma in Paragraphs

Add commas where they are necessary in the following paragraphs.

     The people who developed the Internet never imagined it would be used by so many and they are surprised by the variety of uses people have devised for it. For example people use the Internet to communicate because unlike the Postal Service the Internet can transmit information within seconds. Using their computers users can order many different kinds of products. The Internet unlike most stores is always open. When students need up-to-date information some turn to libraries; others the Internet. Once logged on students can access Web sites that will provide the information they need. People in all walks of life depend on the Internet and people of all ages use it. Business people and political leaders are logging on; likewise senior citizens and young children. The Internet has changed the world of communication.

Lesson 3 **Using Commas for Clarity**   *Application*

A. Proofreading for Comma Usage

Insert this proofreading symbol ⌄ to add commas where they are needed. Cross out any commas that are not necessary. Use an ✗ or this delete symbol ◞.

Turning on her computer Brooke first checks her e-mail. She has two messages. One is from her cousin; the other a forward. Her cousin wants Brooke to attend the same school as she. Brooke unlike her twin sister, Gina does not know which college she will attend after she graduates from high school. The message from her cousin not the requests from her sister prompts Brooke to look at colleges on-line.

Many of her friends want to go to colleges that are nearby but Brooke thinks she would like to see another part of the country. The Internet is a great tool for Brooke can find schools that offer programs, in International Affairs. The bigger schools not the smaller ones tend to have the programs she likes. But the big schools usually have very large classes; the small schools smaller classes.

Since Brooke is interested in schools, that are far away, she cannot visit them all. Brooke unlike her friends who toured nearby schools decides to take virtual tours, of the schools on-line. Within a click she can see pictures of each of the buildings on the campuses. Many of the colleges are attractive but they are also very expensive. Brooke uses the computer all afternoon to research colleges; after that scholarships.

B. Writing with Commas

Correct each of these comma splices in three different ways, that is, by splitting the sentence into two sentences, by using a semicolon, and by adding a conjunction. Write your revised sentence or sentences on the line. Draw a star or asterisk by the revision you think is best in each set.

1. Basketball players run almost constantly during a game, they must have stamina.

_____

_____

_____

_____

2. The bus driver saw me waving, he didn't even slow down.

_____

_____

_____

_____

Other Comma Rules

Teaching

Use a comma in these situations:

- to set off a personal title or a business abbreviation
  Michael Brown, Sr., is my father.
- in the salutation of a personal letter and the closing of any letter
  Dear Grandmother,   Your grandson,
- between the day of the month and the year, and, in a sentence, after the year
  Carla was born in Chicago on February 17, 1987, and moved here last year.
- to separate the street, city, and state in addresses and names of places
  The company is located at 3596 Monticello Blvd., South Euclid, Ohio, in a brick building.
- in numbers of more than three digits to denote thousands
  The trip odometer registered 1,215 miles.
- to set off a direct quotation from the rest of the sentence
  "Come right in," the manager said.

Using Commas Correctly

Insert commas where necessary in the following sentences.

1. "Meet me at the movie theater in an hour" Katie said.
2. On October 20 1998 my sister celebrated her twenty-first birthday.
3. "Play your best" the coach told us.
4. The new car our family bought cost $15000.
5. The letter was addressed to Jacob Edward Beethe Jr. at my home address.
6. Dear Mr. Graham Sr.

   I enjoyed meeting with you last week. Our discussion was most enlightening. I look forward to the next time we meet.

   Yours sincerely
7. My work address is 41 Orchard Drive Lexington Massachusetts and is only a block from the grocery store.
8. Pablo joined a health club on June 15 1996 and has worked out every week since.
9. There are 5280 feet in a mile.
10. The candidate said "I will be the next president of the United States."
11. Harold Lacy Ph.D. is the winner of the Nobel Prize for Chemistry.
12. Mei's parents were married July 28 1986 and she was born exactly four years later.
13. The new shopping mall will be built at 1500 Wilson Court Lincoln Iowa but won't be completed till next year.
14. Brendan runs almost 1100 miles a year, training for the cross-country team.
15. My grandfather is James Tyler Sr. and my father is James Tyler Jr.

Lesson 4

Other Comma Rules

More Practice

A. Using Commas Correctly

Add commas where necessary in the following sentences.

1. Hawaii became a state on August 21 1959.

2. Claire Robertson M.D. will speak at the conference next week.

3. Our house at 319 March Circle Arlington West Virginia has a spiral staircase.

4. The library has our local newspaper on microfilm from January 1 1922 to the present.

5. Michael Jordan was the second player to score over 3000 points in a season.

6. My favorite clothing store has moved to 125 South Street Portland Indiana.

7. Dear Maria

 My family is moving to your area. Our new address is 1977 Union Blvd. Silver Spring Maryland. We will be able to see each other more often now.
 Your friend

8. The drama coach announced "Kayla will play the lead in the school play."

9. In the mayoral race, John Carson garnered 13500 votes, and Kirsten Watson received 24000 votes.

10. The law firm just promoted Alastair Browning Sr. to partner.

11. On August 4 1987 the hotel at 500 Lincoln Street Worcester Massachusetts was torn down.

12. "This concert will be the biggest event of the year" said the radio deejay.

13. Dad's college graduated its first class on June 11 1904 when there was only one building on campus.

14. The house at 1313 Hollow Avenue Salem Wisconsin is where they filmed the new horror movie.

15. Jackson and Leigha were born February 2 1992 in the middle of a blizzard.

B. Using Commas in Paragraphs

Add commas where they are necessary in the following paragraph.

 The great inventor Thomas Alva Edison was born on February 11 1847 in Milan Ohio. Largely self-schooled, he went to school for only three months in Port Huron Michigan. And yet this energetic man is responsible for some of the most useful inventions ever made for example the electric light bulb and the phonograph. When quite young Edison learned how to work the telegraph and armed with that skill landed a job in Boston Massachusetts. Selling his first invention an improved stock ticker earned him the whopping sum of $40000. With that money, he was able to open his own laboratory in Menlo Park New Jersey; he later moved his lab to West Orange New Jersey. On November 20 1877 Edison made history. He shouted "Mary had a little lamb." Why were those words so significant? He said them into a funnel on a primitive phonograph marking the first time sound had ever been recorded and reproduced. All in all Edison patented over 1000 inventions. The "Wizard of Menlo Park" died on October 18 1931 in West Orange New Jersey.

Other Comma Rules

Application

A. Proofreading for Comma Usage

Insert this proofreading symbol ⋀ to add commas where they are needed.

We would like to think that invention is easy and spontaneous. The truth is much less romantic. Indeed, the process of invention usually involves hard work and years of experimentation. Wilhelm Conrad Roentgen Ph.D. a physics professor, had been investigating cathode rays for quite a while. Although he made other important discoveries, he is best remembered for his November 8 1859 accidental discovery of X-rays. Similarly, Charles Goodyear, after working for years in New Haven Connecticut to find a substitute for rubber, accidentally dropped sulfurized rubber onto a hot stove. The resulting compound turned out to be what he had been looking for all along. You might say "It was just luck." But was it luck or was it hard work that made these discoveries possible?

B. Writing with Commas

Write a news article about an imaginary interview with an eccentric inventor. In your article, include the following situations where a comma is needed: a personal title, a date, a complete address, a number of more than 999, and a direct quotation.

_____

_____

_____

_____

_____

_____

_____

_____

_____

_____

_____

Apostrophes

Lesson 1

Teaching

Follow these guidelines when using apostrophes to form possessives:

- for a singular noun or an indefinite pronoun, add an apostrophe and an *s*, for example, *one nurse's cap* and *anybody's guess.*

  Exception: You often add just an apostrophe when using the singular possessive form of classical and biblical names ending in *s*, for example, *Jesus' followers* or *Hercules' strength.*

- for a plural noun that ends in *s* or *es*, add only an apostrophe after the final *s*, for example, *two nurses' caps , the Joneses' award.*

- for a plural noun that does not end in *s*, add an apostrophe and an *s*, for example, *children's book.*

- if the names of two or more persons are used to show separate ownership, add an apostrophe and an *s* to each name, for example, *Yoshi's and Megan's reports.*

- if the names of two or more persons are used to show joint ownership, add an apostrophe and an *s* only to the last name, for example, *Yoshi and Megan's project.*

- for a compound noun, add an apostrophe and an *s* to only the last part of the noun, for example, *mother-in-law's visit*

Other uses of apostrophes include the following:

- Use an apostrophe to show the omission of letters in contractions, for example, *he's* meaning "he is"; or to indicate the missing digits in a year number, for example, *'98* (but not to form plurals of dates such as centuries, as in *1800s;* but never to form a possessive pronoun, such as *yours, hers, his, its, ours, theirs,* or *whose*).

- Use an apostrophe to form the plurals of letters, numerals, abbreviations, and words used as words, for example, *C's, 10's, M.D.'s, yes's.*

- Use apostrophes to show where sounds have been omitted in poetry or in dialect, for example, *'bout, s'pose, ain't.*

Any punctuation that follows a word ending with an apostrophe should be placed after the apostrophe. This treatment departs from the usual rule, which dictates that a period or comma be placed within other punctuation. For example, *She favors the lawyers' , but I prefer the judges' .*

Using the Apostrophe

On the line at the right, write the possessive form of the boldfaced word or words, or else write the contraction that can be made from the two words that have been boldfaced in each sentence.

1. **Someone** lunch has been in this refrigerator four days. _____

2. Our dog **does not** bark at anyone except the mail carrier. _____

3. Three **doctors** offices were crowded with patients. _____

4. His **father-in-law** dog is trained to visit patients in hospitals. _____

5. **Al** and **Steve** computer club attracted 15 new members. _____

6. After its initial rejection, **Lois** painting slowly gained acceptance. _____

7. Shirley wants to become a **children** librarian someday. _____

8. **Lauren** and **Anthony** short stories both appeared in a national magazine. _____

Apostrophes

Lesson 1

More Practice

A. Using the Apostrophe

Underline any words that need apostrophes or apostrophes and *s*'s in the following sentences. Then, above each underlined word, write the word correctly.

1. Matt been doing weight training exercises, but he isnt ready for competition yet.
2. Charise books, Liza jacket, and Tess loafers were crammed into the small locker.
3. In the early 1900s, men and women clothing differed greatly from styles of today.
4. Our literature class is comparing Ezra Pound and T.S. Eliot poetry.
5. The teachers admission tickets are red, while the students tickets are blue.
6. In the last election, the yes outnumbered the no by a three-to-one margin.
7. Wasnt the class of 01 donating a new trophy case to the school?
8. Another person solution to the physics problem may be just as valid as yours.
9. The Volunteers Club collected ladies clothing and children toys for the homeless shelter.
10. Mr. and Mrs. O'Donnell admired their daughter-in-law new car.
11. Did you find Charles key or Ed homework in your car?
12. My little sister has trouble writing her *8*s and *2*s.
13. Lee and Kim science project won first prize in the regional competition.

B. Using the Apostrophe Correctly

Rewrite each sentence, adding apostrophes where necessary.

1. I cant tell you for sure what their fate was since historians opinions differ.

   _____

2. Make sure youre on time to the surprise party being held at Jordan and Ashleys house.

   _____

3. The players and the coachs salaries are directly connected with their performances, Im sure.

   _____

4. In three hours time, well be in sunny Puerto Vallarta, Mexico, sitting under poolside umbrellas.

   _____

5. Ive heard that the president-elects first priorities are choosing a cabinet and then straightening out the economy.

   _____

   _____

CHAPTER 10

Apostrophes

Application

A. Proofreading for Correct Punctuation

In the following paragraph look for words in each sentence that require apostrophes and, possibly, *s*'s. First underline them and then write those words correctly on the corresponding lines below. If no words in a sentence require apostrophes, write **Correct** on the line.

(1) The photographer use of a camera as a means of artistic and social expression began in the mid-1800s. (2) The worlds first aerial photograph, a balloonist view of Paris, was Gaspard Felix Tourachan most famous achievement. (3) Julia M. Cameron's often fuzzy portraits of Charles Darwin and others nevertheless captured her subjects' personalities. (4) During the 50s and 60s, various people photographed Europe and America historical sites and natural features. (5) Auguste and Louis Bisson pictures atop Mont Blanc are remarkable. (6) Once seen, Matthew Bradys photographs of the Civil War cant be forgotten. (7) His pictures captured the battlefield horrors as well as the soldiers humanity. (8) In the late 1800s, William Jackson photos of the West helped gain the necessary yes in Congress to establish the world first national park, Yellowstone. (9) Jacob Riis views of urban slums helped to highlight and eventually improve one of New York City worst districts. (10) Needed children's labor laws resulted partly from Lewis Hine's photos of youngsters working in coal mines and factories.

1. _____   6. _____

2. _____   7. _____

3. _____   8. _____

4. _____   9. _____

5. _____   10. _____

B. Writing with Correct Punctuation

Follow the directions to write and punctuate sentences correctly.

1. Write a sentence that uses an apostrophe to show possession in a plural noun ending in *s*.

_____

2. Write a sentence that uses an apostrophe to show possession in a singular noun.

_____

3. Write a sentence that discusses joint possession by two people and uses apostrophes appropriately.

_____

4. Write a sentence that discusses separate possession by two people and uses apostrophes appropriately.

_____

<table>
<tr><td></td></tr>
</table>

Hyphens, Dashes, and Ellipses

Teaching

Here are ways to use hyphens (-), dashes (—), and ellipses (. . .).

Hyphens Use a hyphen to connect words, word elements, or the parts of a compound word, as follows:
- in compound numbers from twenty-one to ninety-nine, and in fractions such as *two-thirds*
- in certain compound nouns, such as *mother-in-law, great-grandson*
- in compound adjectives used before (but not after) the noun it modifies, such as *best-known candidate*
- in words with the prefixes *ex-, self-, quasi-,* and *all-,* and with the suffix *-elect*
- to avoid confusion or to avoid repeating a vowel or consonant, for example, *pre-election, cell-like*
- when part of a word must be carried over from one line to the next (Words should be divided only between syllables. Keep at least two letters of the hyphenated word together on a line. Divide an already-hyphenated word at the hyphen, and never divide a one-syllable word.)

Dashes Use dashes for the following reasons:
- to signal an abrupt change or an idea that breaks into the thought of a sentence
  Specials—at least according to regular patrons—are excellent.
- to set off explanatory, supplementary, or parenthetical material in sentences. The salads available—house, Caesar, and Cobb—are all delicious.

Ellipses Remember the following guidelines for using ellipses (also called ellipsis points).
- Use three ellipsis points to show that one or more words have been omitted within a quoted sentence.
  "The critics are raving about . . . this film."
- Use a period and three ellipsis points to show that quoted material, such as the following, has been omitted: the last part of a sentence, the first part of the following sentence, an entire sentence or more, or an entire paragraph or more.
- In fiction or informal writing, three ellipsis points may also be used to indicate that an idea or a character's voice trails off.

A. Using Hyphens and Dashes

Write the correct form of the boldfaced word, including hyphens, on the line. Add dashes where they are needed. If no additional punctuation is needed, write **Correct.**

1. Filled dumplings—Polish pierogi, Italian ravioli, Jewish kreplach, and Chinese won ton are an **alltime** favorite food around the world. _____

2. The pastry chef a **greatgranddaughter** of the creator of the Waldorf salad carefully piped the cream rosettes onto the eclairs. _____

3. A delicious caramel **crystallike** glaze was drizzled over the flan. _____

Lesson 2 # Hyphens, Dashes, and Ellipses   *More Practice*

A. Using the Hyphen

In these sentences, underline each word that requires a hyphen, and write the corrected word on the line at the right.

1. Raspberry fudge was voted the mostliked ice cream flavor of the month.

   _____

2. In the election for class treasurer, I received thirtyfour more votes than my opponent.

   _____

3. The selfproclaimed automotive genius ran out of gas on the way to school this morning.

   _____

4. Joshua's sisterinlaw gave him a Labrador retriever for his birthday.

   _____

5. Governorelect Williams enjoyed attending county fairs around the state.

   _____

B. Using Dashes in Sentences

Rewrite each sentence inserting dashes where they are needed.

1. Talking animals, evil witches, elves, and fairies all these characters are commonplace in fairy tales.

   _____

2. It was all my fault no, I take that back the fault was partially yours.

   _____

3. All of your nervous habits tapping your fingers, cracking your knuckles, and scratching your head are getting out of hand.

   _____

4. This painting if I must say so myself is my best work to date.

   _____

C. Using Ellipses

Read the following passage. Then choose the passage below in which ellipses points have been used correctly to quote the passage. Circle the letter before the correct passage.

> The Ship Island region was as woodsy and tenantless as ever. The island has ceased to be an island; has joined itself compactly to the main shore, and wagons travel, now, where the steamboats used to navigate.
>
> Mark Twain, *Life on the Mississippi*

1. The Ship Island region was as woodsy. . . . as ever. The island. . . . has joined itself compactly to the main shore, and wagons travel, now . . .

2. The Ship Island. . . . has ceased to be an island . . . and wagons travel, now, where the steamboats used to navigate.

Lesson 2 — Hyphens, Dashes, and Ellipses *Application*

A. Proofreading for Correct Punctuation

Indicate where hyphens (-) or dashes (—) are needed in the following paragraph.

> **EXAMPLE** Which are the best known restaurants in our city? Your opinion, not to mention my own, means the difference between their success or failure.

A look in the phone book under *Restaurants* produces a mindnumbing array of choices. Whether *haute cuisine* or fast food, there is a restaurant to match every taste. Some establishments specialize in certain types of food seafood, barbeque, steaks and chops, or vegetarian. Other places are best known for their ethnic flavor. Anyone and her greatgrandmother can sample distinctive European cuisine French, Italian, German, Polish, Greek in a wide variety of locations. In addition to the everpopular Chinese food, there are subtly different tastes of the Far East Japanese, Thai, Korean, Vietnamese. Indian, North African, Middle Eastern, and Mexican exciting flavors and textures abound. Not that hungry? Look for a coffeehouse with its specially blended coffees and teas Colombian, Arabica, or English black. If all else fails, get a pizza!

B. Using Ellipses

You want to quote the following passage from *The Joy Luck Club* by Amy Tan, but you have room for only four lines. Read the passage and decide which words or phrases you can omit and still maintain the sense of the paragraph. Rewrite your revised paragraph on the four lines below. Use ellipses to show where you have omitted words.

> My mother spread out an old striped bedspread, which flapped in the wind until nine pairs of shoes weighed it down. My father assembled his long bamboo fishing pole, a pole he had made with his own two hands, remembering its design from his childhood in China. And we children sat huddled shoulder to shoulder on the blanket, reaching into the grocery sack full of bologna sandwiches, which we hungrily ate salted with sand from our fingers.

_____

_____

_____

_____

Lesson 3

Semicolons and Colons

Teaching

Use a **semicolon** to join the independent clauses of a compound sentence in which no coordinating conjunction is used; between independent clauses that are joined by a conjunctive adverb or transitional phrase; between independent clauses joined by a conjunction if either clause contains commas, and to separate items in a series if one or more of the items contain commas.

> Gems are minerals used in jewelry; their beauty determines their value.

> Gems are not always ready to use; in fact, some gems look rough and dirty in their natural state.

> Most diamonds, considered by some to be the most beautiful of gems, come from Africa; and the best pearls in the world come from two places, the Persian Gulf and the South Pacific.

> Some gems are made by humans; others are found in igneous, metamorphic, or sedimentary rocks; and still others are organic in origin.

Use a **colon** after an independent clause to introduce a list of items; between two independent clauses when the second clause explains or elaborates the first; and to introduce a long or formal quotation.

> Diamonds are mined in these areas: Australia, Africa, and Russia.

> Gems can be quite valuable: some cost millions of dollars.

> A gem expert has written this about the Cullinan diamond: "The beauty and clarity of this diamond is beyond compare. Imagine a diamond that weighs more than 3,100 carats—equivalent to about 1,000 diamonds typically used in rings."

Use a colon in these additional ways: after the salutation in a business letter (*Dear Sirs:*); between numerals indicating hours and minutes (*6:15*); and to separate numerals in references to certain religious works, such as the Bible and the Talmud (*Luke 5:4*).

Using the Semicolon and Colon

Add semicolons and colons appropriately to the following sentences.

1. The British Crown Jewels include the following St. Edward's Crown, the Orb and Scepter, and the Coronation Ring.

2. Many gems are minerals or stones however, amber is a fossil resin used as a gem.

3. A stone must be hard enough to last a long time only stones ranking seven or higher on Mohs' Scale will wear well.

4. Most turquoise is found in areas of little rainfall the American Southwest contains a sizable quantity of this gem.

5. The value of a stone depends on its rarity but color, hardness, and brilliance also are very important.

6. Several imitation gems are composed of a soft glass, called paste some are produced in a lab and others, doublets, are made by gluing small stones together.

7. Emeralds, jasper, and carnelian are mentioned in Revelations 4 3.

8. The travel brochure stated "When you visit Washington, D.C., spend time at the Smithsonian. See the fabled Hope Diamond and a dazzling array of other gems."

CHAPTER 10

Lesson 3

Semicolons and Colons

More Practice

A. Using the Semicolon and the Colon

On the lines, write the word from each sentence that should be followed by a semicolon or colon. Then write the correct punctuation mark that should follow the word. If a semicolon or colon is needed within a numeral, write the entire numeral plus punctuation.

1. We drove through Wolf, Wyoming, Salt Lake City, Utah; and Reno, Nevada.   _____

2. The snow is falling heavily we should be able to ski tomorrow.   _____

3. I like reading in fact, I read at least a book a week.   _____

4. The sermon centered on a quotation from Proverbs 4 12.   _____

5. The garden is filled with beautiful flowers violets, daisies, and roses.   _____

6. To whom it may concern   _____

   Please send me your latest catalog.

7. Ken wants to be a teacher therefore, he plans to major in education at college.   _____

8. Victor found the book, read it, and took notes then he began the book report.   _____

9. He quoted Isaac Bashevis Singer "When you betray somebody else, you betray yourself."   _____

10. Our tour included the following a wax museum, an art gallery, and a library.   _____

B. Using the Semicolon and the Colon in Writing

Add semicolons and colons where they are needed in these paragraphs.

(1) Walk past any jewelry display case the gem most likely to catch your eye is the dazzling diamond. (2) Diamonds are the hardest materials found in nature thus, they are the longest wearing of all gems. (3) These stones are highly prized in addition to hardness and brilliance, their rarity adds to their value.

(4) There are four known diamond fields in the world Africa, India, Russia, and South America. (5) Most diamonds are mined in Africa the country of South Africa produces the majority of these gems.

(6) Some of the largest, most flawless diamonds ever found are world famous the Cullinan, the Koh-i-noor, the Regent, and the Hope. (7) The Cullinan, weighing one and one-third pounds, is the largest diamond ever found it was cut into nine large stones and 96 smaller ones. (8) Both the largest of the Cullinan stones and the Koh-I-noor are now part of the British crown jewels the Regent is the property of the French government. (9) The Hope diamond is notable for its deep blue color it can be viewed at the Smithsonian in Washington, D.C.

Semicolons and Colons

Lesson 3

Application

A. Writing Sentences with Semicolons and Colons

For each item, write the sentence that is described in parentheses.

> **EXAMPLE** (sentence that uses a semicolon to join the parts of a compound sentence without a coordinating conjunction)
> *The dance instructor was frustrated; she had never encountered anyone with such a lack of rhythm before.*

1. (sentence that uses a semicolon before a conjunctive adverb and a comma to join clauses in a compound sentence)

_____

_____

2. (sentence that uses a colon to introduce a long quotation)

_____

_____

3. (sentence that uses a colon to introduce a list of items)

_____

_____

4. (sentence that uses a semicolon to separate parts when commas appear within parts of a series)

_____

_____

B. Proofreading a News Article

The reporter who wrote this news article was in a great hurry. He omitted both semicolons and colons. Prepare the article for publishing by adding needed semicolons and colons.

Each month of the year has a precious or semiprecious stone associated with it these gems, called birthstones, are considered lucky. Some people think the idea of birthstones originated with a Bible story however, no one can be sure. The story describes a breastplate decorated with 12 precious stones this vestment belonged to Aaron, the first high priest of the Israelites. Ancient writers connected the 12 stones to the 12 months of the year thus, the birthstone was born.

Gems in deep red and purple colors mark the months of January, February, and July garnet, amethyst, and ruby are the respective birthstones. March, September, and December gems are varying shades of blue the stones are aquamarine, sapphire, and turquoise. The yellow-green peridot is the birthstone for August the golden topaz marks the month of November. No list would be complete without diamonds, emeralds, and pearls people born in April, May, and June can claim these gems. Rounding out the list is the mysterious opal, the birthstone for the month of October. Whether harbingers of good luck or not, birthstones add color and beauty to our world.

Quotation Marks and Italics

Teaching

Lesson 4

Quotation marks set off direct quotations, titles, and words used in special ways. Follow these guidelines when using quotation marks and italics:

- Use quotation marks (" ") at the beginning and at the end of a direct quotation. Do not use quotation marks to set off an indirect quotation. Punctuate a speaker's words with a period, comma, question mark, or exclamation point inside quotation marks.

  Kyle asked, "What quotes from Benjamin Franklin do you remember?"

  Enclose both parts of a divided quotation in quotation marks. Do not capitalize the first word of the second part unless it begins a new sentence.

  "He wrote so many," Cindy answered, "in *Poor Richard's Almanac*."

- The first word of a quotation introduced by words such as she said is capitalized.

  She said, "I've finished my literature review."

- Use a comma to replace an ending period before words such as he said.

  "I want a vegetarian pizza," he said.

- Put colons or semicolons outside the closing quotation mark.

  His words have been described as "pithy": they are concise.

- Use single quotation marks when you write a quotation within a quotation.

  "I've always remembered these words, 'There is no little enemy,'" said Bill.

- If the quotation consists of more than one paragraph, begin each paragraph with a quotation mark; do not use a closing quotation mark until the end of the entire quotation.

- Use quotation marks to enclose the titles of short works and works that are contained within longer pieces, such as magazine articles, chapters, short stories, TV episodes, essays, poems, and songs. Use them to enclose slang words, unusual expressions, technical terms, and definitions of words.

- Use *italics* for titles of long works—books, newspapers, magazines, works of art, TV series—and for names of vehicles—ships, trains, aircraft, spacecraft. Also, italicize unfamiliar foreign words or words referred to as words. When writing by hand or using a typewriter, use underlining to indicate italics.

Writing Sentences with Quotation Marks and Italics

Add quotation marks, commas, and end marks where necessary in each sentence. Also underline any word that should be italicized. If the sentence is correct, write **Correct** on the line.

1. Have you read the poem The Love Song of J. Alfred Prufrock by T. S. Eliot? _____

2. As the French would say, I am very au courant when it comes to popular music. _____

3. The words nuance and entourage have come to us from the French language. _____

4. Do you need my help? the secretary asked. _____

5. The postcard reads, Wish you were here, said Margie. _____

6. One reviewer called the musical pathetic; another labeled it innovative. _____

7. Sara confided, Then he whispered, I'll always be your friend. _____

8. "Don't jump around so much," warned Jesse, "or you'll overturn the canoe." _____

CHAPTER 10

Quotation Marks and Italics   *More Practice*

A. Using Quotation Marks

Add quotation marks, commas, and end marks where necessary in each sentence or conversation. Underline any word that should be italicized. One sentence is correct as is.

1. Ashley said, In his book Poor Richard's Almanac, Benjamin Franklin says, Three may keep a secret if two of them are dead; I've definitely found that to be true.

2. One of Franklin's proverbs states If you would not be forgotten, as soon as you are dead and rotten, either write things worth reading, or do things worth the writing.

3. I like the inscription on Franklin's gravestone said Alice. There Franklin wrote in part: The Body of Benjamin Franklin, Printer . . . will . . . appear once more, in a new and more beautiful edition, corrected and amended by the Author.

4. My mom always quotes Franklin's proverb He that riseth late must trot all day Tom declared ruefully.

5. Franklin also wrote: Reading makes a full man, meditation a profound man, discourse a clear man.

6. Sylvia reminded the group that other people had said or written words worth remembering.

7. Sylvia continued, Think of the words of Booker T. Washington, author of the book Up from Slavery: I shall never permit myself to stoop so low as to hate any man.

8. Finally she added let's remember Robert Benchley's remark: Drawing on my fine command of language, I said nothing.

B. Using Quotation Marks in a Dialogue

Add quotation marks, commas, and end marks where necessary. Underline any words that should be italicized.

Grasping Poor Richard's Almanac in her hands, Pilar read, He that falls in love with himself will have no rivals. Benjamin Franklin really knew how to say a lot in just a few words, didn't he she said. I would like to write something people would quote, too she sighed.

That's not easy to do exclaimed Lisa. It takes skill and hard work to write well. Thoreau in his Journal wrote A perfectly healthy sentence is extremely rare.

Yes, I know writing is difficult said Pilar. I read that F. Scott Fitzgerald, author of the novel The Great Gatsby, once noted: All good writing is swimming under water and holding your breath. Even so, I'd still like to be a famous writer.

Lisa retorted, In the words of Oliver Wendell Holmes, who wrote the poem The Chambered Nautilus, Fame usually comes to those who are thinking about something else.

Then, I think it's time to finish my homework Pilar replied, and maybe practice my rim shots.

Lesson 4

Quotation Marks and Italics   *Application*

A. Correcting Misuse of Quotation Marks and Italics

Rewrite the following sentences, using quotation marks, commas, and end marks correctly. In your rewritten sentence, underline any words that should be italicized.

1. "Did you see last Sunday's episode of World of Sports? asked Tracy. I thought it was fascinating."

_____

_____

2. "I caught the last half-hour, when the reporter interviewed that skier replied Jason. "Could you believe it when she said "I'd ski even if I had a broken leg?"

_____

_____

3. Tracy said, 'I saw an article about her called 'Extreme Skiing" in my latest copy of "Sports Around the World."

_____

_____

4. "She believes that she is "destined for greatness;" she tries to ignore the danger of her sport said Tracy."

_____

_____

5. "I'm not even sure what the terms schussing and traversing mean, but I love to watch skiers on TV", said Jason. "Sometimes I think I should try that sport myself"?

_____

_____

B. Writing with Quotation Marks

Write a dialogue for a short story about two friends who meet each other after a long separation. Make sure that you indicate clearly who is speaking. Use quotation marks and other punctuation marks correctly. Include one word, phrase, or title that should be italicized. Use a separate piece of paper, if necessary.

_____

_____

_____

_____

CHAPTER 10

Lesson 5

Parentheses and Brackets

Teaching

Use **parentheses** ( ) to enclose supplemental information in a sentence or text. When parenthetical material occurs within a sentence, do not capitalize the first word or end with a period. You may, however, end with a question mark or exclamation point.

> The new sci-fi movie **(have you seen it?)** has great special effects.

Put punctuation marks after the closing parenthesis, not before the opening parenthesis.

> The main character **(a fighter pilot)**, can see the future.

Punctuate and capitalize a parenthetical sentence that stands by itself as you normally would.

> I predict the movie will be a box-office success. **(We all went to see the previous one in the series, didn't we?)**

Use **parentheses** to enclose figures or letters that introduce items in a list within a sentence and to set off numerical information such as area codes.

> I enjoyed the movie for these reasons: **(1)** great special effects, **(2)** exciting plot, and **(3)** stirring theme.
> Alice Wonder can be reached at **(123)** 456-7890.

Use **brackets [ ]** to enclose an explanation or comment added to quoted material and in place of parentheses inside parentheses.

> One viewer commented, "That guy **[the fighter pilot]** could really fly a plane!"
> See the movie at a theater near you. (A list of theaters is printed in your local newspaper **[see page C-10]**.)

A. Using Parentheses

Place parentheses where they are needed in the following sentences.

1. Expressionistic art art that expresses the strong inner feelings of the artist was popular in the early 1900s.

2. Among artists who are considered expressionists are 1 Vincent van Gogh, 2 Edvard Munch, and 3 Wassily Kandinsky.

3. Violent colors and elongated figures these are common characteristics of expressionism are used to provoke strong emotional reactions.

B. Using Brackets

Place brackets to follow the directions for each sentence.

1. "P. Phineas T. Barnum possessed incredible business savvy." (Explain that Barnum's first name was Phineas.)

2. "She Babe Didrickson was one of the greatest woman athletes of all time." (Explain that *She* refers to Babe Didrickson.)

3. "This bus the one to the Broadview Mall never comes on time." (Explain that the bus being referred to is the one that goes to the Broadview Mall.)

CHAPTER 10

Lesson 5

Parentheses and Brackets

More Practice

Using Parentheses and Brackets

Rewrite each sentence using parentheses or brackets.

1. Some movie stars are in demand for these reasons: 1 their acting ability, 2 their box-office potential, and 3 their "likability" quotient.

_____

_____

2. We had no trouble getting tickets for the new horror film. After seeing the movie, I can understand why.

_____

_____

3. Concessions for example, popcorn and cola cost a lot more at the multiplex than they do at the grocery store.

_____

_____

4. The lawyer said, "Recall the court's recent ruling the one regarding censorship when you make your decision."

_____

_____

5. A good trivia question who could answer it? would be to name the best supporting actor from last year's awards.

_____

_____

6. Important jobs in the motion-picture industry include the following: 1 director, 2 cinematographer, 3 costume and set designers, and 4 editors.

_____

_____

7. According to a recent poll, popcorn is the favorite food of moviegoers. (A complete list can be found in *Poll Word* see page 14.)

_____

_____

CHAPTER 10

Parentheses and Brackets

Application

A. Using Parentheses and Brackets

Rewrite each sentence by adding or replacing parentheses or brackets.

1. Animated movies are complicated to make for these reasons: 1 all "actions" must be drawn sequentially, 2 many artists are needed, and 3 individual "cels" sheets of transparent celluloid must be produced frame by frame.

_____

_____

2. Famous movie dancers Fred Astaire comes to mind were some of the more popular movie stars of their time.

_____

_____

3. Silent movie star Harold Lloyd did all his own stunts. [By the way, in one movie he climbed (reportedly with nothing to break his fall) to the top of a tall building.]

_____

_____

4. The respected newspaper critic Marilyn Graham wrote of the film: "In all my years on the job, (Ms. Graham has been a movie critic for 15 years) this was worst movie I have ever seen."

_____

_____

B. Writing with Parentheses and Brackets

Write a sentence using each of these parenthetical expressions. Use the expression either within the sentence or standing by itself.

can you believe it?   see appendix A   wouldn't that be great?

my personal hero   outlining civic goals   an old wives' tale, probably

_____

_____

_____

_____

_____

_____